JUST DO WHAT God SAYS

Dr. Paul C. Brown, Sr.

XULON PRESS

Xulon Press
2301 Lucien Way #415
Maitland, FL 32751
407.339.4217
www.xulonpress.com

© 2021 by Dr. Paul C. Brown, Sr.

All rights reserved solely by the author. The author guarantees all contents are original and do not infringe upon the legal rights of any other person or work. No part of this book may be reproduced in any form without the permission of the author.

Due to the changing nature of the Internet, if there are any web addresses, links, or URLs included in this manuscript, these may have been altered and may no longer be accessible. The views and opinions shared in this book belong solely to the author and do not necessarily reflect those of the publisher. The publisher therefore disclaims responsibility for the views or opinions expressed within the work.

Unless otherwise indicated, Scripture quotations taken from the King James Version (KJV) – *public domain*.

Scripture quotations taken from the New King James Version (NKJV). Copyright © 1982 by Thomas Nelson, Inc. Used by permission. All rights reserved.

Paperback ISBN-13: 978-1-6628-2162-2
Ebook ISBN-13: 978-1-6628-2163-9

Table of Contents

Dedication vii

Introduction ix

Chapter 1: Just Do What God Says 1

Chapter 2: "Timely Devotional Thoughts"
Vera's Life Verse: Habakkuk 3:17-19 13

Chapter 3: Vera: Wife, Mother, Woman of God 29

Chapter 4: The Joyful Homemaker 54

Chapter 5: Women in the Home 59

Chapter 6: Remembering and Honoring Mom. 67

Chapter 7: One, Two, Three, into God's Presence 94

Chapter 8: Treasured Memories 100

Chapter 9 The Word of God has No Expiration Date 133

Dedication

I want to dedicate this book to my children: Carmela, Paul Jr., Patrick, Renita, and David. You have been an inspiration to me. As I write about your Mom, I reflect on all of what she poured into each of you. What you have become has a direct bearing on your Mom's investment in your lives. The apostle John writes, "I have no greater joy than to hear that my children walk in truth" (3 John 4 NKJV). Your mother and I thoroughly enjoyed raising you five. I pray you will continue to honor God and keep Him the center of all your decision-making. I also pray you will emulate the principles and concepts your mother has instilled in each of you. Remember her life statement and verse: *"Just Do What God Says"* (Habakkuk 3:17-19). That is your rallying cry and marching orders. Keep Pressing, my children.

Introduction

Over five decades ago I had the pleasure of covenanting in marriage to Vera Louise Wright. We were blessed of God to remain married for nearly 50 years. Yes, we had a wonderful marriage and were blessed to raise five children. As I have learned over these many years, nothing is wasted in the life of a believer. God was in the center of our home, and we desired to serve Him. As we traveled through life, we would also experience the many challenges that faced families. Yet, as I look back on the life we shared together, I have no regrets.

The last nine years of marriage I became the primary caregiver to Vera who eventually succumbed to dementia. Yet I thank God for the privilege to serve her and hold to the covenant of marriage. Moreover, the centerpiece of this book is a glimpse at her life. Her life statement, *"Just Do What God Says,"* is what she lived and always encouraged others to follow that pattern. I have come to learn that the Word of God does not have an expiration date. What God has promised He is able to perform. We both believed that! Before dementia came along, she had contributed much to the kingdom of God. I pause to write a little about her life and our family. You will hear testimonies from others whose lives were impacted by this woman of God, Vera Louise Brown.

I pray you will be encouraged and hopefully gain further insights regarding what God has called you to do. Remember: There is no expiration date on the Holy Writ. We just need to do what God says. Indeed, I have come to learn that the best place to be is in the center of the perfect will of God. Vera made certain that principle was the centerpiece of our family too. And anyone who came into our home was blessed by the homemaking qualities of Vera. May you be inspired reading a little about her life and legacy.

Chapter 1

JUST DO WHAT GOD SAYS

"Who can find a virtuous woman? For her price is far above rubies." Proverbs 31:10

As believers in Jesus Christ we are called to make a difference for the sake of the kingdom of God. We are called to a higher standard. Indeed God has given us the gold standard of His Word for us to follow. Thus, the statement "Just Do What God Says" was a lifelong phrase embraced by Vera. She was the epitome of ensuring we were stimulated and motivated to honor God's Word through obedience. She made absolutely certain that her family and others with whom she may have conversed, were reminded to "do what God says to do."

In the life of a Christian one is called to be salt and light in a dark and tasteless world. This present world-system refers to the order and arrangement under which Satan has organized the world of unbelieving mankind upon his cosmic principles of ambition, greed, force, pleasure, and selfishness. However, we as believers are born again and alive in Christ to make a difference. God has given us the command to be obedient. From the very beginning as we go back to Genesis, we read instructions given to the man in his unfallen state: And the Lord God commanded the man saying, "of every tree of the garden you may freely eat; but of the tree of the knowledge of good and evil you shall not eat, for in the day that you eat of it you shall surely die." (Genesis 2:16-17) Hence, the standard given by God was well-defined and certain. There is no question regarding the instructions given to the man as to what he was supposed to honor. Nonetheless, the Bible states, "Therefore, just as through one man sin entered the world, and death through sin, and thus death spread to all men, because all sinned." (Romans 5:12) As a result our spiritual DNA was corrupted because of sin; yet, God put in place a way for man to be redeemed. God gave instructions for how a man, woman, boy or girl can get back into a right relationship with Him.

Obedience has been the rim that encompasses the Christian life. There is no other way aside from the standard God has put in place to bring about reconciliation for the lost. From Genesis 3:14-15 we read God giving the Adamic Covenant which conditions the life of fallen man, conditions which must remain until the kingdom age. The elements of the Adamic Covenant are: 1) the serpent, Satan's tool is cursed (v. 14); 2) the first promise of the Redeemer (v. 15); 3) the changed state of the woman (v. 16); 4) the earth is cursed (v. 17); 5) the inevitable sorrow of life (v. 17); 6) the light occupation of Eden (Gen. 2:15) changed to burdensome labor (vs. 18, 19); 7) physical death (v. 19; Romans 5:12-21).

The first promise of a Redeemer is given in Genesis chapter three which points to and is fulfilled in Immanuel-Christ. There is no other way for anyone to get in a right relationship with God other than through Jesus Christ (John 14:6). This is a very grave and crucial point. There is salvation in none other than Jesus Christ the Son of God (John 20:31; Acts 4:12). The battle has been raging over the heart and soul of mankind since the garden in Eden, and this battle will continue until our Lord returns. Therefore, I want to take this opportunity to travel through Scripture to explain the importance of a word that many folks do not like: *obedience*.

Vera had plenty of insight having adopted the phrase and principle "Just do what God says." I praise God for His servant, Miss Vera, as some have called her for years. I thank God for the privilege He gave us to have shared life together, raising godly seeds of children who are sowing back into the kingdom of God. We set out to honor the Word of God in all that we do. As we looked into the Scriptures we learned biblical principles of what God expected of us and we patterned our lives accordingly. The Lord our God honored His Word and blessed us beyond measure. Together we kept pressing!

If I were to mention these names: McCall's, Simplicity, Butterick, etc., what comes to your mind? That's right, patterns. I recall the second appliance we invested in was a Singer sewing machine. I must say many clothing were fabricated as Vera sought to use these patterns, cut out materials, and make clothes for her family. She was a versatile homemaker and used the skills God blessed her with to make a house into a home. Indeed the children and I were blessed by this godly woman who we loved and adored.

Vera and I sought out to live a life that will honor the Lord. From the time we affirmed our covenant in marriage, the will of God became our quest. Early in our married lives we were a bit radical, believing that we could accomplish anything for the kingdom of God. Oh, our faith was strong and we worked together. We were young Christians and beginning to learn what the Christian life was all about. I am thankful for the ones that God sent along to nurture and instruct us in the way. God led us to ministries which were instrumental and integral to our growth in Christ. I am the more grateful to God for the men who spent time discipling me. They instilled a solid foundation of principles in my life. I saw them live out what was in the inside. I in turn would share what I learned with Vera and together we grew and desired more. God would be sure to bring to pass much in our lives, and we had an appetite for spiritual knowledge. Indeed as we opened our hearts and mind God began to teach us, showing us the paths we should take and giving us instructions for raising a family that will honor the Word of God. Life was not always a bed of roses, but we sure made the best of everything God gave us. Yes, we set out to do what

God told us to do. We appropriated Romans 15:4 which says, "for whatever things were written before were written for our learning, that we through the patience and comfort of the Scriptures might have hope."

Hence, we endeavored to discover what was written before and seek to make application of its truths to our lives. "Just do what God says" does go back to Genesis. Yet, throughout all of Scripture we discover men and women of God who followed God's instructions. Let me therefore list several of these and elaborate upon its truth. We both embraced what God required and sought out to do what He says. There is a song we learned years ago that was central to our faith. It is entitled The Bible Stands:

> *The Bible stands like a **rock undaunted** 'Mid the raging storms of time; its pages burn with the truth eternal and they glow with a light sublime. Chorus: The Bible stands though' **the hills may tumble**, It will firmly stand when the earth shall crumble; I will plant my feet on its firm foundation, For the Bible stands.*

This is one verse from this hymn, yet it says much as to what we believe. The Scriptures are foundational to our faith and we patterned our lives according to its principles. The world today says that the Bible is outdated, but as for me and my house we did what God said (Joshua 24:15), regardless of societal norms. God's Word will stand forever (Isaiah 40:8). It is to this end that we followed the Word of God desiring to live a Spirit-filled life and model before our children what God's Word commands. A life lived for the Lord is not in vain. God blessed us with children who are walking with Him. Amen! I recite what the apostle John said, "I have no greater joy than to hear that my children walk in truth" (3 John 4). As I look back over my life and reflect on what God instructed Vera and I to do as parents, I have no regrets. Life was not always easy, but God has allowed me now to see the fruit of our labor. Vera is in God's presence now and what she sowed into the lives of our children was integral to where they are today. To God be the glory!

Now let us move forward to see what some of the patriarchs did with the instructions they had from God. Abram was called the spiritual pilgrim. While in Haran he received his calling from God. In Genesis chapter 12 we read the call of this patriarch. He was instructed to separate and leave his home and go to a new country. Abram did as the Lord instructed and left for a new place. He obeyed the call of God and journeyed onward, being led by God. El Shaddai, Almighty God, appeared to him in Genesis 17 when Abram was ninety years old. He was instructed to "walk before me, and be thou upright or sincere." In response, Abram fell on his face. God talked with him, and his name was changed from Abram to Abraham, for a father of many nations would come from him. God made a covenant (Abrahamic Covenant) with him. Five times we read God saying, "I will" do something for Abraham. It is interesting to note the name El Shaddai. El signifies strong one. Shaddai denotes nourisher, the strength-giver; thus, He is able to make a ninety years old man fruitful. The covenant was confirmed in Isaac. As we follow this patriarch, we see there were four great crises in his spiritual experience: 1) country and kindred, 2) his nephew Lot, 3) his plan about Ishmael, and 4) Isaac, thy son, thine only son Isaac, whom thou lovest" (Genesis 22:2). The focus would be upon Isaac. In Genesis 22 we read the offering of Isaac. God told Abraham to take Isaac to the land of Moriah and offer Isaac there for a burnt-offering. He obeyed God, rising early and in three days came to the place of which God told him. As he laid his son on the altar, stretched forth his hand, and took a knife to slay his son, the angel of the Lord called unto him and instructed him to not do anything to Isaac. God provided a ram instead. The angel of the Lord said, "For now I know that thou fearest God, seeing that thou hast not withheld thy son, thine only son from me" (Genesis 22:12b). Yes, Abraham did what God said. Abraham was justified by faith. "For what saith the scripture? Abraham believed God, and it was counted unto him for righteousness." "He staggered not at the promise of God through unbelief; but was strong in faith, giving glory to God; and being fully persuaded that, what he had promised, he was able also to perform" (Romans 4:3; 20-21). If Abraham was present today he would also say, "Just do what God says." He followed the pattern of obedience!

Another patriarch who followed God's pattern of obedience was Joshua. We learn from him how to be successful in the battle of life. Joshua 1:8-9 states, "This book of the law shall not depart out of thy mouth; but thou shalt meditate therein day and night, that thou mayest observe to do according to all that is written therein: for then thou shalt make thy way prosperous, and then thou shalt have good success. Have not I commanded thee? Be strong and of a good courage; be not afraid, neither be thou dismayed: for the LORD thy God is with thee whithersoever thou goest." Appropriating what God says in His Word is integral to the believer living a life that is pleasing to God. Joshua was discipled by Moses, and when Moses died God commissioned Joshua. This book records the consummation of the redemption of Israel out of Egypt. Four times in chapter one God said to him "be strong and of good courage." It is worth focusing on that statement for indeed God directed and ordered his steps out of Egypt and into Canaan. Earlier when the Israelites came to Kadesh Barnea Joshua was one of the spies who surveyed the land for 40 days. Only he and Caleb were ready to do what God said to go and possess the land. It was said several times of Caleb 40 years later that *he wholly followed the Lord*. Saints of God it is vital that one follow and obey the instructions from God. There is no other option. Joshua led the Israelites in the conquering and division of the land of Canaan. Before his death Joshua gives a farewell address in chapters 23 and 24. A prominent verse is this one, "And if it seems evil unto you to serve the lord, choose you this day whom you will serve; whether the gods which your fathers served that were on the other side of the flood, or the gods of the Amorites, in whose land ye dwell: but as for me and my house, we will serve the Lord" (Joshua 24:15). Oh that we would have husbands, fathers, to take a stand like that, to put God first and separate from the defilement that is in this world's system. Once again we see the pattern laid out by God followed and obeyed by this patriarch who believed God.

Israel would soon lapse back into idolatry after the death of Joshua. There will arise another generation which knew not the

Lord. It is absolutely essential that parents instruct their children in the way of the Lord. This was not the case, and the next generation forsook the Lord and followed other gods and bowed themselves unto them. The same things are happening today as people are giving themselves over to the deception of the enemy: pleasure, ambition, greed, and force. All are satanic. Yet, God is seeking a remnant that will do what he says in spite of the status quo. As one reads the account in the book of Judges, we see a roller coaster effect of up and down. The people lapsed into idolatry. God allowed them to go into captivity. They cried to God and He would send a judge to bring about their deliverance. One of these judges was a man called Gideon. After the fourth apostasy and servitude, the children of Israel cried unto the Lord because of the Midianites. The Lord would send a prophet to tell the people "ye have not obeyed my voice" (Judges 6:10). Thereafter, the angel of the Lord spoke to Gideon, saying, "The Lord is with thee, thou mighty man of valour." God told him, "Go in this thy might, and thou shalt save Israel from the hand of the Midianites: have not I sent thee?" (Judges 6:12b, 14). God continued to say, "Surely I will be with thee" (vs. 16). Gideon had an experience with Jehovah-shalom, the Lord send peace. Gideon put forth a fleece of wool and twice God honored his request. Afterwards, Gideon was ready to move forward with God's plan. He started with 32,000 people and God told him it was too many. So, 22,000 who were fearful and afraid were sent home. That left 10,000 and God said again the people are too many. After a test at the water's edge 9,700 were sent home. God said, "By the 300 that lapped will I save you and deliver the Midianites into thine hand" (Judges 7:7a). God wrought a mighty victory that day over the Midianites. It was God's way, God's timing, and God's victory. Gideon followed the pattern God laid out before him, and yes, he did what God said! The saying "Just do what God says" is truly crucial, essential, and necessary for every believer to become victorious.

There are many others whom I may mention that followed God's pattern. One may read Hebrews chapter 11 to see a glimpse of God's hall of fame, those who embraced God's will and were obedient to do what God said. Time will not allow me to discuss them all. However, I must talk about Jesus. Yes indeed "whatsoever was written aforetime, were written for our learning" (Romans 15:4a). Jesus is our prime supreme example of obeying the will of God. He stated, "And he that sent me is with me: the Father hath not left me alone; for I do always those things that please him" (John 8:29). This statement was made as Jesus gave a discourse on his deity. What he said did not sit well with the religious leaders of that time. Yet, He continued in the will of God. I hope that pleasing God will be the aim of every believer. Oh that we would be intentional regarding doing God's will from the heart. Jesus said, "My meat is to do the will of him that sent me, and to finish his work" (John 4:34). Submission to the divine will of God was His focus. He exemplified this in the Garden of Gethsemane when he prayed, "O my Father, if this cup may not pass away from me except I drink it, thy will be done" (Matthew 26:42b). Prayer is essential to seeking and performing the will of God. The Psalmist recites, "Teach me to do thy will; for thou art my God: thy spirit is good; lead me into the land of uprightness" (Psalm 143:10). In this way Jesus becomes our standard. The apostle Paul shared insight regarding the mind of Christ in Philippians 2:5-8, "Let this mind be in you, which was also in Christ Jesus: Who, being in the form of God, thought it not robbery to be equal with God: But made himself of no reputation, and took upon him the form of a servant, and was made in the likeness of men: And being found in fashion as a man, he humbled himself, and became obedient unto death, even the death of the cross." The sacrifice of His life was the ultimate cost in order to redeem us. Jesus Christ was in complete agreement with the Father's will. Yes, He did what God the Father said. Therefore, Christ's example is to be followed. He says, "Take my yoke upon you, and learn of me" (Matthew 11:29a); "If any man will come after me, let him deny himself, and take up his cross, and follow me" (16:24); "For I have given you an example, that ye should do as I have done to you" (John 13:15). Much more could be said, but we are called to follow Christ's example and do what God says!

Vera and I spent much time praying and searching the Scriptures to learn what God required of us. We esteemed and cherished the Word of God. It was central to our home and the prime directive for raising our children. Yearly, we both would travel to Atlanta in preparation for SPOLIWA's board meeting. The night before we would spend time in prayer, anointing each other with oil and setting ourselves apart to hear from God what His plan for us would be for the upcoming year. God honored those times in our lives. "Just do what God says" became our marching orders, and Vera embraced this to the very core of her life. The will of God was second to none. We wanted to ensure we followed

God's Word, listened to the Holy Spirit, and appropriated what we knew God required. I pray beloved that you too would make every effort and endeavor to honor the Lord through a life of obedience. There is no other option. I pray you will have a hunger and thirst to honor the Lord in everything. My encouragement to you beloved is this: "that ye may stand perfect and complete in all the will of God" (Colossians 4:12b). Finally, my brothers and sisters, "Just do what God says."

Chapter 2

TIMELY DEVOTIONAL THOUGHTS

Vera's Life Verses: Habakkuk 3:17-19

"Though the fig tree may not blossom, nor fruit be on the vines; Though the labor of the olive may fail, and the fields yield no food; Though the flock may be cut off from the fold,

And there be no herd in the stalls:
Yet, I will rejoice in the Lord,
I will joy in the God of my salvation.
The Lord God is my strength;
He will make my feet like deer's feet,
And He will make me walk on my high hills."

· · · · · · · · · · · · · · · · · · ·

January 2, 2002 – John 13:1-10

Never say never because the Lord is the one who will direct my path. Lord help me to trust you to direct me. Thank you Lord for bringing me this far in my life! A man's heart plans his way but the Lord directs his steps (Proverbs 16:9). It's snowing today, oh, how beautiful.

· · · · · · · · · · · · · · · · · · ·

January 22, 2002 – Mark 1:29-39.

Sometimes I am so busy with trying to do so many things. Stop and take time to pray and seek the Lord through His word. Jesus took the time to get alone with the Father. Vera takes the time to be with the Father. Meet God in the morning if you want to walk with Him through the day.

January 24, 2002 – 1 Timothy 6:10

Caught in a current! Help me Lord to stay in your will. It is so easy to drift away from God's truth, regular worship and a life of faith. The compass, God's Word, will keep me from spiritual shipwreck.

··················

March 9, 2002 – Mark 12:13-17, 28-31

Lord help me to use my time and my money wisely. Lord help me to give you more of my time and whatever money I have to you. Thank you, Lord, for what You are doing in my life.

··················

March 14, 2002 – 1 Samuel 13:1-15

So many things can happen when we are disobedient to what the Lord would have us do. It could cost us our very home, job or even our lives. Help me Lord to do what you say in Your Word. ("Just do what God say do")

··················

March 15, 2004

Lord, help me to take care of my physical heart as well as my spiritual heart. Help me think, speak, and behave as the Lord will have me to. Am I keeping spiritually fit? Weight-lose the weight of unnecessary burdens and cares; Pulse-maintaining a steady rhythm of gratitude of praise; Blood Pressure-is my trust greater than my anxiety? Diet-am I enjoying the life-giving nutrients of the Word of God? I need to keep checks on my heart; to keep spiritually fit consult the Great Physician, Jesus.

· · · · · · · · · · · · · · · · · ·

March 18, 2004

Thank You Lord for listening to me when I talk to You. You hear my cries and you know what I need to hear from You. Help me to be slow to speak and quick to listen.

· · · · · · · · · · · · · · · · · ·

March 30, 2004

Help me to live a life that is alive for the Lord. I don't want to be a dead Christian! Lord, stir up the fire in my life!

· · · · · · · · · · · · · · · · · ·

March 31, 2004

I thank you Lord for speaking to my heart. I thank you Holy Spirit for opening my heart and ears to hear your voice...Roger and Jean came to visit us. I thank you Lord for letting us see each other's face again. May the Lord continue to bless and keep them always. Thank you for bringing us across their paths.

September 22, 2004 – Matthew 14:14-21

Lord, help me to show compassion to others along the way because you have shown compassion to me. Without Jesus I can do nothing. You Jesus always showed compassion (Love in action). Help me to be moved with compassion towards others: "Compassion is Love in Action."

· · · · · · · · · · · · · · · · · ·

September 24, 2004 – Proverbs 16:1-9

I thank you Lord for directing my way. Sometime I make the wrong turns but Lord even in that because you are guiding me, it's alright. The "*stops*" of a good man are ordered by the Lord as well as his steps.

· · · · · · · · · · · · · · · · · ·

September 30, 2004 – Psalm 119:129-136

Lord, teach me your statutes and please direct my steps according to your Word. Give me a heartfelt desire to read your Word every day and <u>obey it</u>.

October 1, 2004

Lord, help me to forget and forgive others who have hurt me in my pass along the way of life. Lord, let me remember kindness; let me be kind to others even when they are not kind to me.

· · · · · · · · · · · · · · · · · · ·

October 4, 2004 – Daniel 3:1-18

Lord, help me to trust you even when things won't go the way I desire. I must trust in you in spite of the trials that may overwhelm me.

· · · · · · · · · · · · · · · · · · ·

October 13-14 2004

I need to start sharing your Words with others. Let me be a shining light so others then may view your mercy and your love displayed in all I say and do; because I have not been doing it. Help me to point people to Christ; please let that be my mission for you; so many broken lives. Lord, help me to tell of your love for mankind – a love for the sin-sick, the broken, blind and help them to see by the way that I live a wholeness of being that You long to give!

October 19, 2004

Lord give us (me) grace to trust you when life's burdens seem too much to bear. Dispel the darkness with new hope and help me rise above despair; no one is hopeless whose hope is in the Lord. Thank you, dear Lord.

．．．．．．．．．．．．．．．．．．．

October 25, 2004 – 2 Timothy 4:6-8

What am I living for? I look forward to the day when Jesus will say "well done my good and faithful servant; you lived and served well."

．．．．．．．．．．．．．．．．．．．

November 2, 2004 – Titus 3:1-8

Today is the day that the country voted for new officers in our country. Christians can be constructive if they refuse to be destructive. Lord, help me to be a good citizen. I voted today. I have done my duty; God bless America!

．．．．．．．．．．．．．．．．．．．

November 9, 2004 – Acts 16:16-31

God's son can brighten my darkest days. God often sends me joy through pain, through bitter loss divinest gain; yet through it all dark days or bright I know my Father leads aright. God has a purpose in our heartaches. The Savior always knows what is best. We learn so many precious lessons in every sorrow, trial and test. When you trust in God pain is an opportunity for progress.

• • • • • • • • • • • • • • • • • •

November 22, 2004 – Matthew 5:13-16

Christians should lead exemplary lives. But it is important that we reveal the source of strength and life, which enables us to be different. As Jesus said, "Let your light so shine before men, that they may see your good works and glorify your Father in heaven. Like a brightly shining light in darkness of the night we will stand for truth and right. Let the whole world know it is the life behind the words that makes your testimony effective. Lord may others see Christ in me. I want to be a better light for you Jesus. I don't want to be a "closet Christian."

• • • • • • • • • • • • • • • • • •

December 1, 2004 – Romans 7:14-25

Struggling is a part of living. Nothing's gained on flowery beds of ease. But when our hearts are set on Jesus, struggle drives us to our knees. If Jesus lives within us, sin need not overwhelm us. Can't get fixed when you're dead!

December 16, 2004

Honor your father and mother that thy days may be long upon the land which the Lord thy God give you. Thank you, Lord, for my mother and all she has done for me. My mother was a wonderful Lady. She loved her children very much. She did all that she could to help us be the best we could be. She went through much in her short time of life. Thank you, Lord, for a wonderful mother. She was always giving to others. My mother loved my husband Paul as if he was her own child. Paul loved my mother as if she was his mother. I hope that I can be half the woman she was. Thank you Lord for my mother. I pray that my children will say the same about me.

....

January 6, 2005 – Habakkuk 3:17-19

Lord, forgive me for not being thankful for all you have done for me. Lord, help me to be thankful for all that have come my way. You could have let me be even sicker so Lord I thank you for the cough. I could be on my death bed but you have kept me. Help me to trust you through all I have faced, but there are others who are going through much more than me. Thank you Lord. Help me be like Arthur Ashe. He died not stop trusting God. Lord you are a great God. I will trust you with all my heart.

January 7, 2005 – Romans 1:8-17

I owe all to you Lord for paying my debt by dying on the cross for me. You took my place so Lord I want to say thank you for my salvation paid in full. Lord, thank you for it all. Help me to do the same to others. I <u>must</u> tell them that you love them and you gave your life so that they might live. We could never repay the Lord for salvation, but that should not stop us from showing our gratitude. We are indebted to him for everything. The least we can do is show our appreciation by telling others about him. Jesus gave his all for us (me). Do we give our all for Him? Do I give my all for Him?

. . . .

January 11, 2005 – Ecclesiastes 1:1-11; 12:13-14

Fear God and keep his commandment for this is man's all. It is a great thing to be alive.

Thank you, Lord. It is exciting to think about the eternity God has for us (me). It sure is great to be alive. Life can be depressing when God is left out, but how exciting it is when He is at the center. When we focus on Christ everything else becomes clear. Is Christ on the throne of your life? Have you peace, love and joy what no power can destroy? Is Christ on the throne of your life? YES!

January 19, 2005 – Psalm 119

Today is a special Day for me. This day I have been married to Paul for 36 years. He has been my dearest and loving friend for all this time. I am 54 years old and on February 5, 2005 I will be 55 years old if the Lord let me live. For these past 36 years Paul has been the best Friend that I have ever known next to the Lord. My sisters and my children friendship are so important, but Paul has been here for me through many hard times. When I have been sick or down hearted God kept me. Thank you, Lord, for friendship but the best companion is you. We all need someone to love and someone to love you. Christian fellowship promotes spiritual growth!

....

January 24, 2005 – Read Job 29

We may look at ourselves as good, but God sees the inward man. From a human perspective many people may be described as good, but God sees the disobedience, selfishness and hate that lie deep within all of us. He also knows that we have spiritual blind spots and when we open our eyes we see ourselves as He does. We understand why a good man like Job said, "He abhorred himself. Lord, help me to be good, but never lose sight of my sinfulness and unworthiness. Thank you for the forgiveness you offer in Christ. Even the best people have nothing to boast about save Jesus Christ.

January 27, 2005 – Luke 9:18-26

Christianity in modern America tends to be easy, upbeat, convenient, and compatible. It does not require self-sacrifice, discipline, humility, an otherworldly outlook, a zeal for souls, a fear as well as a love of God. If we were only customers of Almighty God we could be selective in our faith and reject anything we did not like. But that's not an idea we get from Jesus. He pointed to a cross not to a spiritual check-out counter. (Luke 9:23-24) Christ died on a cross for our sins not for our satisfaction. We must trust him and follow him. In a world where the customer is always right it takes radical obedience to God to keep from buying into consumer Christianity. Following Jesus is not always easy, but it is always right!

· · · · · · · · · · · · · · · · · · ·

February 1, 2005

Four days from my birthday and I will be 55. Thank you, Lord, for allowing me to live these many years! My prayer is that I will live a life for Jesus Christ. The Lord saved me many years ago and I am so happy that I am saved, but I want to be a blessing to others and to see others come to Jesus Christ. This lesson meant so much to me. A clear call I heard from God: come to Jesus and I did. Tell others what Jesus has done for me. He saved me and made me His child. A life lived for God leaves a lasting legacy. *When God calls be willing and ready to listen!*

February 2, 2005 – Colossians 1:3-8

Three days before my birthday and look at me complimenting myself! Lord, help me to compliment others and not myself. Help me to be ready to thank others for the great things that they do. Encourage my husband for caring for me and going with me to see the doctor. I thank him for taking the time to sit and talk with me when I am going through things in my life. How do I respond when someone commends me? Why is it sometimes hard to accept a compliment? Do I freely praise others for their accomplishments? *Praise loudly; blame softly.*

· · · · · · · · · · · · · · · · · ·

February 11, 2005 – 1 Corinthians 13:4-7

Lord help me to be aware of the way I may speak to others. Help me to say kind words that will build up someone and not tear them down. Help me to be kind and to be mindful of how I want to be treated. Help me to apologize to anyone that I may hurt. Help me to remember what Christ has done for me when I was wrong in sin. Help me to be aware of what I may say. Lord, help me to have a kind word to say a word of strength to build someone else up. *Help me to pray first.*

February 16, 2005 – 1 Peter 5:6-11

"May the God of all peace after you have suffered a while perfect – establish, strengthen and settle you." While we wait for comfort, we can be assured that God will not allow us to be tested beyond our ability to bear the trial. It is screened through his perfect love. We will not suffer one moment more nor will we suffer more intensely than is necessary. There may be fires through which the core of your character must pass. *But in the midst of them God promises to be your partner, companion and faithful friend.* He will perfect, establish, strengthen and settle you; and then when He has finished his work, he will take you home to heaven and wipe away all your tears forever (Rev. 21:4). Tears are often the telescope by which we can see into heaven.

. . . .

February 23, 2005 – 2 Kings 7:3-9

Most times we run to tell others about bad news but take our time to tell the good news that could help someone. This was the story in this lesson. When the king of Syria laid siege to the city of Samaria the food supply was cut off. Four men with leprosy deciding it would be preferable to die at the hands of the Syrians than to starve went to surrender to the enemy. But when they came to the camp, they found it deserted. The army had fled in the night; food lay everywhere. The four men stuffed themselves and they tempted to remain silent about the good news. They said we are not doing right. So, they became evangelist bearers of good news. Ultimately evangelism comes down to this: *"one starving person telling another starving person where they can find food."*

....

May 10, 2005 – 2 Samuel 12:13-23

We are so lovable we want God to answer "yes" every time but there are times when God says NO; even when we think that God should say yes! David fasted and prayed to the Lord day and night for his son's healing. In spite of his sincere petitions the baby died. Instead of behaving like a demanding child and being angry with God, David got up, washed, changed his clothes, went to the house of the Lord and worshipped.

....

July 22, 2005 – Genesis 41:46-57

When we go through difficult times it is best to trust God to see us through because God can cause us to be fruitful in the time of our affliction. Thank you, Lord! God will cause our hearts not to be bitter. If we accept adversity enduring every pain; then we will learn what we should know our grief will turn to gain. Adversities are often blessings in disguise. This is the month when the house flooded! Thank you, Lord! You have taught us to trust you. Thank you, Lord!

"...God has poured out His love into our hearts by the Holy Spirit, whom He has given us." Romans 5:5 (NIV)

. . . .

July 28, 2005 – Psalm 103:2

"Bless the Lord, O my soul, and forget not all His benefits." We often take God's blessing for granted until they are taken from us. Then we recognize how important even the most common gifts of God really are. Because God's goodness is as constant as the sun, we are in danger of forgetting what He showers on us each day. If we count our blessings one by one, we'll never get finished. But if we jot down a list of 10 or 20 gifts God gives us each day, something will happen to our hearts. Every morning as we rise God's new mercies greet our eyes and when twilight shadows fall evening blessings brighten all. If you want to be rich, count all the things you have that money cannot buy.

Chapter 3

VERA: WIFE, MOTHER, WOMAN OF GOD

"Favor is deceitful, and beauty is vain; but a woman that fears the Lord, she shall be praised." Proverbs 31:30

As I reflect over these past 50 plus years, so many moments and memories come to mind. One of the exciting times I recall is when I shared my faith with Vera. She being moved by the Holy Spirit after having heard the Word responded by receiving Jesus Christ as Lord and Savior. This was indeed a time to remember as we both celebrated her birth into the family of God, and we proceeded to becoming one in Christ. We did not know what experiences awaited us, but God did. January 1969 would be a most memorable month for us to include salvation, covenant in marriage, and Christ becoming the center of our lives.

At this time in our lives I had been six months in the United States Air Force attending tech school at Sheppard AFB, Texas. Vera had just started matriculation at Roper School of Nursing in Charleston, South Carolina. By the way, Charleston is home for both Vera and me. Most of our families still reside in the Charleston area. Thus, my time home on leave was limited. Yet, we made the best of the time we had and were the more encouraged about this new life we sought to share together. Our daughter, Carmela, was in the mix, and we endeavored to raise her in a godly manner. This would be our approach to family as we sought to learn more about parenting and all that it entails.

If you were a betting person, you may have given us 3-6 months before our flare would soon flicker and go out. But God! We discovered God had a plan for our lives (Jeremiah 29:11, "For I know the thoughts that I think towards you, says the Lord, thoughts of peace and not of evil, to give you a future and a hope.").

We would come to know and experience this verse in time. It did not matter what others thought; we desired to please God and keep Him the center of our family!

I soon returned to tech school resulting in our being apart. We both would focus on our studies. I graduated in the spring and was reassigned to Randolph AFB, Texas. Vera would visit in the summer while her mother took care of Carmela. We were grateful for that time of being together. Vera returned to school, and I became more work oriented and began discipleship with Roger Witteveen. There was a small group of us guys under Rogers's guidance, and I learned a lot. I observed how he led his family. Roger demonstrated what a godly husband should do, and that season was extremely helpful to me.

As time moved forward the year would come to an end. I gained much insight studying God's Word as I was being discipled. God poured much into my life during this season. Vera completed nursing school in December and soon after I received notification of an assignment to a remote base in Southeast Asia. We discussed spending the next seven months together. Roger and Jean opened their home to Vera, Carmela, and me. We stayed with the Witteveen's for about a month. Afterwards we rented an apartment for the next five months. Living together in our first apartment would teach us many things.

I was only an Airman First Class "two-striper." Money was very tight, and we were paid monthly. Vera was good at managing what funds we had. There was one month we ran out of money one day before payday. We did not inform anyone that we were "broke" and needed financial assistance. That day we ate gravy, onions, and bread for dinner. I felt defeated, but she was an encourager. As I reflect on so many years ago, I thank God for my wife who was very prudent and reminded me that God will make a way for us.

We thanked Roger and Jean for the many insights they shared and modeled. Vera and I would emulate much of what we saw in their home.

We left for Charleston as I prepared to go to Southeast Asia. This would be during the height of the Vietnam War. Vera was about four months pregnant. We located an apartment which rented for $65 monthly. After purchasing furniture I needed two months' rent for a deposit. I contacted the Air Force Aid Society which loaned us $130. We thanked God for their assistance.

Before leaving for the remote assignment, Vera was offered a job at Roper Hospital. We thanked God for providing. It would be a long year, and God would teach us both many principles during this time. This godly wife and mother would be vigilant to take care of our home. In December Paul Jr., was born. I received a Red Cross notification of his birth that mother and baby were doing fine. Vera's mother, Dorothy, would take care of Carmela and Paul while Vera was working. Vera attended Shiloh AME Church during her stay in Charleston. I thanked God for her hunger for the Word to ensure our children received sound biblical instruction. In the meantime God was working on me. I made a lordship decision in March 1971 to completely surrender my life for God's disposal.

It was a difficult time being apart, but God kept us faithful during this season. There were no iPhones back then. We spoke via the Mars Station. They would get a connection stateside in the early morning, send a runner to get you and you would go to the Mars Station, put on a headset, sit in a closed booth and speak to your wife. As we spoke the guy in the station would be listening to our "mushy conversation." After I completed a sentence I had to say "over" so the station manager would transfer through the switch so

Vera could talk. We didn't care; we were just glad to talk as often as we could.

While in Thailand I was approached by someone in a cult, and Vera was approached by someone in a cult back stateside as well. This religious group rejected the very foundation of our Christian faith, the deity of Christ. Yet, I thank God for the spiritual foundation He gave to us as we severed ties with them. Not everything spiritual is of God. We would come to know more of this as the years come and go.

Upon returning stateside I was reassigned to Robins AFB, Georgia. It was so good seeing Vera after being apart for a year. We spent a lot of time together. Carmela had grown so much, and Paul Jr. was about 6 months. It was so wonderful to be reunited with my family. Vera and I took a trip to Warner Robins to locate a house or apartment. We were fortunate and blessed of God to find a two-bedroom house which rented for $75 per month. Thanking God for a fruitful trip we returned to Charleston to prepare to move. Vera had to resign her nursing position as we prepared to move to Georgia. We prayed for God's will regarding this relocation. We learned to always make certain that God was in the center and formula of our decision-making. Vera would say, "Let's just do what God say." This statement would become her life declaration!

We rented a truck, packed our belongings, and headed to Warner Robins, wondering what adventures awaited us in this new place. I transitioned into a new job, and things went well. Vera stayed at home with Carmela and Paul Jr., and we started attending the base chapel for the next several months.

Early fall she became pregnant with child number three with a June due date. Her plans to go back to work were a concern for us. We prayed much about this decision. The Lord spoke to our hearts, and Vera decided to stay at home. Her becoming a homemaker would change things for us financially. However, she desired to be at home with the children. Our desire to raise a godly seed through our children became a primary concern. She did not want a daycare or nursery raising her children. So, she gave up her career in nursing and was contented being a homemaker. We agreed on this decision, and there was never a second thought. The Scripture states, "Can two walk together except they agree?" (Amos 3:3). I am thankful for the oneness God gave us.

Vera was very industrious. She used her giftedness in many ways which were beneficial for our family. Although our income went from two to one, although we were about to have our third child, and although I would be the primary breadwinner, she was very resourceful and used godly wisdom to manage our home. God never allowed the barrel of meal and oil to run dry. The virtuous woman Vera was and her faith in God made our home a happy and joyous place to retreat to after a busy workday. I appreciated her being thrifty and wise in managing our resources. She was an excellent cook, homemaker, seamstress, and much more. Her training in beauty culture would enable her to work from home. Our home was always kept very clean, and every area in some way was useful.

The New Year, 1972, would present new opportunities for us. Vera's sister, Elizabeth "Lizzie," would come and live with us for a while. We also became members of Community Bible Church, which was a part of SPOLIWA Ministries. This ministry would become integral to our continuing growth and service for Christ. We were blessed being under the teaching and leadership of Pastor Thomas and Mrs. Lorraine Carstarphen. Decades later I am still actively involved in SPOLIWA Ministries.

Additionally, our third child, Patrick, was born in June. Vera and I were then faced with the decision to either separate from the military after four years, or I could seek cross-training. We prayed about this decision and were led to remain in the military. I was afforded the opportunity to cross-train into clinical laboratory sciences. We located a three-bedroom house and moved in August 1972. I wanted to make certain my family was stable while I attended technical school. Vera remained in Warner Robins with the children. However, after my being away at school for a few weeks, Vera requested we be together, and I agreed that it would be prudent for us to be together. The school afforded me leave to return and make provisions to move my family to Wichita Falls. We placed our furniture in military storage, and we all piled into our 1963 Ford Galaxy for the trip to Texas. While in phase one training for four months, Vera managed the home in an exceptional manner. She poured into our three children during this time. I must say that there were defining moments raising them, and she was the epitome of a godly mother. She made our home attractive and relaxing. I often thanked God for this godly and wise woman He gave me. While living in Wichita Falls we affiliated with a local church. Yes, we made certain fellowship was an integral part of our family life. I appreciated this wise wife and mother for her godly insights. When God has given you a godly and wise woman you learn to listen. You pray together, and you always keep the Lord in the center of decision-making.

I completed my training in December 1972. We left to visit our family in Charleston and to take Lizzie back home. I was reassigned to Carswell AFB, Texas, for Clinical Laboratory phase two training. While in transit we connected with the Community Christian Church. While there Vera and Carmela were baptized. It was a busy nine months of schooling for me, yet as a family we did many activities. The next summer Vera's sister, Joy, came to spend time with us. It was great having her visit with us. As summer was nearing an end, Carmela would be going to first grade. After learning we would be assigned to Shaw AFB, South Carolina, we were excited and looked forward to being near our hometown. Therefore, we allowed Carmela to return with Joy, and Joy saw to Carmela's enrollment at Rhett Elementary School.

I soon completed my phase two laboratory training and would be reassigned to the hospital at Shaw AFB, Sumter, SC. We left Fort Worth with great anticipation as to what we will experience at this new location and a new job for me. We did not have much time for visiting with family in Charleston as I needed to get processed into my new duty assignment and Carmela needed to be enrolled in a new school.

Vera and I spent much time in prayer during these transitional periods. We sought God's direction and learned early on to include Him in our decision making. Vera, the homemaker she had become, was very innovative to ensure that our home would be a place where we could resort to become refreshed. Carmela attended school daily, and Vera spent much time instructing Paul Jr. and Patrick. It was a new season for us, but we were engaged for what would be some defining moments in family, career, and church.

We attended the base chapel for a while. I connected with a men's bible study on Tuesday nights. It was at this study I met some friends associated with the Navigators, a ministry which focus was discipling men and women in the faith. During a Christmas drop in at the Navigator representative's home I met Pastor Jack Spears of Shawview Presbyterian Church. Our family united with this church in January 1974 and grew significantly under this ministry. It was during this season that we realized we needed more in our Christian life as a couple and family. God had placed us there for this season. Pastor Jack had a love for God and a strong desire to see souls saved and grow in the faith.

To enhance our marriage Vera attended a class entitled The Virtuous Woman, and I attended The Challenge to Christian Manhood. We learned greatly. God revealed principles to us that we embraced, and they were integral to our having a blessed marriage and raising godly children. Our view on many areas of our Christian life was challenged, and we endeavored to make what changes were needed. God knew what we needed, and the timing was absolutely a blessing as we gleaned much information that enabled us to be godly parents, improved our relationship as husband and wife, and allowed us to model Christlikeness wherever we went.

Vera, being the godly wife and mother, was very industrious and made certain our home was a Christ-centered one. The kids and

I appreciated her commitment as mother and wife. She invested immeasurable time raising our children and had a love and heart for God. She desired to see her children grow in their faith. She ensured that the home environment was one where our children could open up, be themselves, ask any question, and not feel threatened. She challenged each of our children to use their God-given gifts and talents, encouraging them to never limit themselves, that they could aspire and achieve whatever they set their heart and mind to do, and to always keep the Lord in their decision making. She was truly admired by her children and to this date they are grateful for their mother's investment in their lives.

I was blessed to be ordained as an elder at Shawview Presbyterian Church. Vera became a Sunday school teacher. She always had a heart for children, to share the gospel, and to see souls saved. She never was one to hold back giving godly instruction to whosoever. God used her in many ways to lead other men, women, and children to Christ. It was our desire to see souls come to Christ.

Vera was invited to lead a women's bible study in Sumter, and she eagerly embraced this opportunity to teach God's Word to a group of women. We had no idea that God was setting the groundwork for us to move further in ministry. These ladies became committed and developed a hunger for more. When the season for this study was completed, I was asked to lead a bible class. Annette Thompson, one of the ladies in the study, inquired with her church and they allowed us to use their educational building on Friday nights. This group was called the "Friday Night Bible Study." God used this season, having equipped both Vera and me to minister His Word and provide a healthy setting for discipleship.

Vera's hunger and thirst to see others come to Christ was very contagious. The bible study began outreach and souls were being won to Christ. We also took many youth to SPOLIWA Bible Camp during this season and many came to Christ. As I said before, Vera had a strong desire to share the gospel.

After several years of ministering at the Friday Night Bible Study, we were moved of God to start a church. We shared this vision with our church family that God was leading us to begin launching a church in Sumter under SPOLIWA Ministries, Inc. So, we informed the Bible study group and asked each one to pray to God for direction regarding being a part of this new church. In March of 1979 New Life Bible Church was organized. Vera was one of the original founding members. She lent her skills to serve where needed: Sunday school teacher, song leader, evangelism team leader, and more. We all wore several hats as we served and was excited about what God was doing with a "handful" of folks. I often said that we were radical "back then."

As we both led the New Life Bible Church ministry, we continued as parents to ensure our children were being raised in a godly manner. They were involved in school functions, extracurricular activities, and the like. Carmela had an interest in learning piano; thus, she began taking piano lessons. This would prove very insightful. When we launched the church she became our musician. There is nothing like being "homegrown" for God's kingdom. God would use this investment in her life for years to minister through her musical skills. Vera realized that God had given us special children, who in time would come to know the Lord and be used of Him in various ways in ministry. We would continue the family altar where we would spend time in family devotions weekly and give each one of the children an opportunity to share. Vera's insightfulness would be integral in allowing the children's individual growth and development. She made certain she catered to each child's temperament, yet she sought to apply godly principles in raising our family. Yes, even during this season she would say, *"Let's do what God says."* During this season another child would be born to the Brown's household. Renita Dorothy Brown came along in August 1981. It would be nine years since Patrick's birth. Now a new baby girl entered our lives. We were all excited.

God would keep us in the Sumter area for nine years. We labored at New Life for three-and one-half years. Others came alongside to serve in this little church, little in numbers, but big in their quest to know Christ and to make Him known. As I look back, I have seen many come out from this church to go further in ministry to make a difference for Christ. Sister Vera Brown would be instrumental in preparing and encouraging others to grow and make a difference for Christ. We labored at New Life until November 1982 when we received military orders for Germany. I prayed and was led of God to leave the church under the leadership of Nate Brock, who would later become pastor.

Leaving New Life would be bittersweet for us both, having established close ties with so many during our time in the Sumter area; yet we looked forward to what God would do with this new move. One must always put the Lord first and involve Him when making decisions. As we relocated to Europe, the members of New Life and the relationships we had established over those nine years would be with us forever. We knew that God would take care of His church.

November 1982 finds us traveling to Wiesbaden, Germany. My military role there would be NCOIC of Microbiology at Wiesbaden Medical Center. This assignment would be a paradigm shift, something completely new. We had plenty of questions: What will we do ministry-wise? Where will we worship? Who does God have for us to meet? What did He want us to do? "Doing what God says" was always central to our moving forward. The children were excited about this new move to another country; they had great expectations too. Until base housing became available, we lived in the Amelia Earhart Hotel until February 1983. While there, we started attending the Lindsey Air Station Chapel.

In February we were offered base housing in the Aukamm Military Community. Here we would reside until the fall of 1985. Vera ensured that our home was comfortable. She took pride in decorating, and it was a wonderful thing to see her handiwork. I recall one winter during the Christmas season. She and I were in our kitchen. Nat King Cole sang the Christmas Song, so Vera took some chestnuts and placed them in the oven. In a little while we heard what sound like an explosion. Yes, chestnuts were meant for an open fire, not the oven. We had a good laugh. There was always laughter in our home, and I thank God Vera made our home a place to retreat, a place where our children can share their thoughts, ideas, hurts, and successes. It was a godly home.

While stationed in Wiesbaden, the Lord allowed us to meet and make some lifelong friends: Earnest and Joann Parish, Craig and Gloria Robinson, Curtis and Shirley Jones, and the Sephus family. We spent loads of time together. We worshipped at Camp Perry Chapel and supported the evening gospel service at Wiesbaden Hainerberg Chapel. Through these two services God would do some wonderful things. Carmela eventually became choir director for the gospel service. God used her talents in music in a wonderful way. I recall one time during rehearsal she pulled her mother aside and told Vera that Vera cannot sing everybody's part in the choir. Well that was an interesting episode, yet her mother received the instruction and went on. Again, our children were instructed to always do what God said. What God allowed us to pour into their lives, they in turn shared back with us.

The Brown, Parish, Robinson, and Jones families always spent time together. I recalled Gloria saying that she and Joann would spend hours with Vera, sitting in the car in front of our home and listening to Vera share principles and insights with them about marriage and family; how they should be as wives and mothers. These women today do thank her for sharing her heart with them. I had the privilege of sharing with Earnest and Craig. I praise God for those years spent in Wiesbaden in that they were predestined by God. Both Earnest and Craig are in ministry today, serving the Lord with gladness. They stated recently that they stayed in trouble. They said, "Paul was always doing stuff for Vera. Then Joann and

Gloria would say we should do the same." I laughed when I think of their statement. Yet, these brothers I am certain would have it no other way. We thanked God for the time He allowed us to spend in Germany. I rejoice to this day that God allowed Vera and me to minister and serve these families in this way. To God be the glory!

Well, three years is not a long time. I was offered the opportunity to remain in Germany for another three years, but the family decided they wanted to go "back to the world." So I turned down the offer to remain and accepted a new assignment stateside. The time drew near for us to leave Wiesbaden. We shared so many tears as we were leaving families who became life-long friends. We would be relocating to a new area. There would be a new church family. We saw God leading us and would be ordering our steps as to where to fellowship. I recalled Pastor Jack Spears saying, "God used the military to transport His people around at the military expense." Well it appears to be somewhat true as we served the Lord wherever we were assigned. There were always opportunities to make Christ known. We left Germany in November 1985 traveling to Whiteman AFB, Missouri. We stopped in Charleston for a brief stay with our families and friends. About a week later we headed to the mid-west. We stopped in Kentucky to spend the night and awakened excited about the next day trip to our new assignment. I met a gentleman in the hotel lobby who inquired about our destination. I told him where we were going, and he responded that there was an ice storm in that location. I informed the family, and they did not seem so thrilled about that weather report, but we kept pressing. The demographics changed the further we traveled west.

As we journeyed Vera was always optimistic and keeping the children happy and encouraging them not to worry, that we would be at our new assignment soon. We exited off I-70 west to highway 65 South. There was snow everywhere, yet the roads remained cleared. We came into the city of Sedalia and saw that Knob Noster was about twenty miles down highway 50. The further we journeyed west the more snow and ice we experienced. When we arrived in the little town of Knob Noster there was ice everywhere and on everything. I looked at my son Paul Jr., and said, "Welcome to the world, my son." This new assignment would not be like Wiesbaden, but God would use it to grow us as spiritually, as a family and individually.

Upon arriving at Whiteman AFB, we lived in base billeting for a while. We were advised that it will be a couple of months before housing become available. Therefore, we rented a mobile home in the meantime. Vera was the epitome of a genuine homemaker. She made the mobile home appear like a castle. I can truthfully say that she invested a lot of time into making certain the atmosphere of our home was peaceful. She devoted herself to spend time with each of our children. We both were committed to raising a godly seed. Our children would be a reflection of Vera and me, yet as they developed spiritually and intellectually, we encouraged their individuality. Vera capitalized the time in working with each one of our children. The children would testify today that they appreciated their mother giving up her nursing career and becoming a homemaker. In doing so, she was able to spend quality time with each of them. The principles outlined in Scripture, specifically Proverbs

22:6 and Ephesians 6:4, were integral to the family's growth and development. I thank God for what He enable us as parents to do in training our children.

The time spent in Missouri would bring to our family new horizons. Soon after we settled in we united with Shiloh Baptist Church in Warrensburg. I was blessed to work alongside Pastor Melvin G. Eaves. As we have been trained to serve our Lord Jesus, we made a commitment to serve in Sunday school and bible study. Yes, the children were in attendance and God used them there as well. Carmela was attending Lander College in South Carolina for her first year of higher education. After the first year she transferred to Central Missouri State University in Warrensburg to be closer to family. Paul and Patrick attended Knob Noster High School. Renita was in pre-school at that time. After a few months of being in this new location God would soon bless our family with child number five, David. His birth would bring a new dimension to being parents for us.

Twenty-one weeks into her pregnancy Vera started spotting at home. She was advised to rest and keep her feet up. Very soon her condition worsened. She started to bleed profusely, and I took her to the hospital on the base. She had four successful and trouble-free pregnancies prior, but this would be a new experience for us. She was admitted and her OB-GYN clinician monitored her that evening and ordered four units of blood. She took two units of blood while in the hospital. The baby's heartbeat remained strong. It was decided they needed to transfer her to a medical center. I returned home to advise the children on what was happening and left the other three with Carmela. I was very concerned about Vera and what the outcome would be. She was transferred to Kansas City. While in route, she was given the other 2 units of blood. We lived about 70 miles from Kansas City, and I followed the ambulance westward on highway 50. All of a sudden it made a U-turn. I followed the same; however, traffic was getting between me and the ambulance. As they headed to Blue Springs I did not see when they turned off the highway. I slowed down and prayed. Suddenly the ambulance retreated from a side street and was headed to interstate 70. This is at the height of morning rush hour. As we made our way to the interstate, the traffic gave the right of way to the ambulance but not to me. As we traveled up the interstate the ambulance got further and further away from me, and I lost sight of where it went. I exited the interstate and back-tracked coming back on and traveling westward. Then seeing a hospital sign I exited and followed it to the hospital complex. There were several hospitals in that area. But God led me to Truman Medical Center where I saw the military ambulance. By the time I parked and was directed to where they had taken Vera, she was being prepped for a C-section. Children Mercy Hospital had a team waiting and soon they brought out a baby I had never seen like this before. He was one and one quarter pounds. They allowed me for a brief moment to see him then they whisked him away to neonatal ICU. I stayed until Vera was brought to recovery. She came through the delivery well. While she was resting I went to find the neonatal ICU. This would be a breathtaking experience. I have been in medical nurseries before, but never one like this. There were alarms sounding off, tubes going everywhere and just an overwhelming encounter. They were caring for him and explained what we could expect down the road. You see he was born on August 14, 1986, but his original due date was December 5, 1986. Yes, this would be a trying time for our family, but God is good! We saw his hand at work in all of this.

Vera expressed much concerned about our newborn son. We thought we would have another girl, but God saw differently. In that we were blessed with a boy, we discussed what his name should be. Vera stated, "If he is going to beat this giant of being a premature baby we are going to name him David; indeed he will slay this giant. Thus, he would be called David." We thank God that little premature baby is now 34 years of age. To God be the glory! We held him for the first time in late September. Vera was so very encouraged and wanted the best care for our newborn. We lived over 75 miles from the hospital and would visit him 3 days per week. On the days we did not visit with him, the nursing staff would call and give us daily updates. We truly appreciated the medical care he received at Children's Mercy Hospital Neonatal ICU. He was so tiny they dressed him in cabbage patch doll clothing; he was a sight to behold. But he was ours. His siblings were excited about their brother.

He grew in the nursery from August until December. They would only release him when he gained 4 pounds. So, on December 5, 1986, which was his original due date, David was released to go home. That was a long way from 1 ¼ pounds! But God! We were excited to leave Kansas City. It was a long four months, but we thanked God for this new day. He was in his own room. We would check on him nightly before going to bed.

On one particular night in February we went to check on him. Vera noticed he looked differently, and she felt something tugging at her heart. Her motherly intuitions told her to pick him up, and we brought him to bed with us. Soon after that He quit breathing. It was a very frantic and panicky moment as things were very confusing. I started breathing for him and instructed Vera to call the emergency room. As I breathed for David he would come around and stop breathing again. This continued until emergency personnel arrived. Thank God we lived on the base not too far from the hospital. They took over, taking David and Vera to the emergency room. I stayed for a moment to get the children settled and they went to the ER. Soon after arriving the ER personnel briefed me on what they had ascertained. Then a laboratory report stated that he had a group B Streptococcus meningitis. Immediately, hospital personnel made arrangements to life flight him to KU Medical center in Kansas City. He was admitted to the ICU. He remained in ICU for about two weeks. While there Vera and I were trained in the use of an apnea monitor. The monitor is designed to monitor the breathing and heart rate of sleeping babies. An alarm goes off if a baby's breathing stops briefly or if the heart rate is unusually slow. While at home David would sleep in his own room once again; however, the alarm would go off repeatedly every time he would move. This made Vera and me very anxious, but we trusted God to bring David and our family through this season. During all this time Vera was stable in faith, believing God would bring her son to manhood and make a difference for Him. The next several years would prove to have its own flavor of challenges, but we trusted God to do exceedingly abundantly. She catered to each one of our children in a way a godly and wise woman would. They appreciated all of her insights and counsel, even when she did not agree with them, they understood that their mom had their best interest on her heart. She was a virtuous woman on so many levels.

The next several years we would see our oldest, Carmela, get married; Paul and Patrick would go off to college at South Carolina State University, leaving Renita and David, to make their mark. I am thankful God has blessed us with godly children who to this day are walking in truth (3 John 4). Much could be said about their godly mother who invested quality time with each of them. I praise God for all He did through Vera's virtuousness.

Going through some photos recently I came across a statement written by our son Patrick. He had just left from home for his first year in college. He wrote in a manual entitled A Place to Stand. One of the pages was entitled, "Advice from Mom." Pat completed the statement: And my mom said to me: *I love you, read your Bible and trust in God always. When you leave this house take what I've taught you and use it. Think before you take action."* WOW! These were some very powerful words of wisdom deposited into our son. Yes, he indeed has appropriated what his mother told him.

As time proceeded we spent the next five years busy serving our great God. Carmela was married and Paul and Patrick went in college leaving Renita and David to enjoy the next phase of family life. I often chuckle to myself. Vera and I began life as young parents, knowing somethings; yet we were still in need of much more. We were rather strict with our three oldest children, yet we employed a lot of loving in raising them. As time progressed, she and I learned more regarding parenting and employed a balance between ministry and family. Therefore, Renita and David received their share of discipline, but we were more lenient towards those two. God taught us a lot during those years, and we were humble to listen to the Spirit and do what God told us. Thus, Vera's life-long statement would be "Just do what God say."

We would continue to be used of God in reaching out to others with the gospel. Vera began to matriculate at Georgia Military College by taking a few courses. She enjoyed the challenge very much. We continued our serving at Shiloh Missionary Baptist Church. Serving in ministry was a very important part of our family life. While in Missouri we also kept pace with SPOLIWA. Our hearts were very much in tuned with this ministry and we praise God for leading us there early in 1972. Over the next five years things would be busy; still we prayed about the future. We always invited God into the center of our decision-making. We knew our military time would come to an end, and we began to make plans to transition to civilian life. After much prayer we decided to take an assignment to Maxwell AFB, Alabama. We figured it would be close to Charleston and would afford us time to visit there to determine if we wanted to return for retirement.

We left Whiteman AFB in the fall of 1991 anticipating what God would do through us in this new location. As often, we had made some lifelong friends while in Missouri; however, God was leading us to a new area of service. Soon after arriving in Montgomery we were living in temporary quarters until base housing would be available. In the meantime, we visited several churches in the area. Canaan Hill Missionary Baptist Church was just outside the base gate. After visiting there we noticed they observed Sunday school and had mid-week bible study. We met Pastor Ossie T. Brown, Jr., his wife Sareta, and their daughter, Oslynn. We did not know then what God had in store for us through this ministry. Vera was excited we found a place to worship. We never did a lot of church hopping and thank God for His direction. It was not long after that we united with Canaan Hill as members in January 1992.

We began serving at Canaan Hill and supported the efforts of Pastor Brown. Vera immediately connected with the Sunday school ministry as teacher of young people. She had a heart for youth. She had a passion to see others come to Christ. While at Canaan we stayed committed to SPOLIWA. That summer we took a van load of children to bible camp. For Vera and I this was our true desire. Together we also led a marriage workshop. It was our heartfelt desire to see couples and families live Christ-centered spirit-filled lives. While in the Montgomery area God would give Vera and me many opportunities to facilitate marriage seminars, workshops, and conferences. Vera was sought after on many occasions to speak for women conferences in the Southeast. We thank God for the doors He opened for her in this area of ministry.

The fall of 1993 SPOLIWA Ministries asked us to consider planting a mission church. We prayed and agreed to form Grace Bible Church of Millbrook, Alabama. There were a handful of us, but we thank God to be able to proclaim Christ's gospel through this ministry. While at Grace we stayed associated with Canaan Hill. God had given us great favor with that ministry as well and opened doors to other churches in Millbrook. Vera as always encouraged us to "just do what God says do."

We were blessed of God to travel the southeast and minister God's Word together. It was a joy to see her in action as she proclaimed Jesus Christ. I am thankful reflecting over the many ways God used the two of us. The Christian Women United invited her on several occasions to be a keynote speaker at their conferences. God allowed her to flow in His grace and knowledge as she ministered to women. After nearly six years of serving through Grace Bible Church, we felt of God it was time to let go of this ministry. We were gracious for Aundrey and Nadine Wingate, Paulette Hale and her children, and Costella Harris and her girls, who served with us there. We thanked God for the season He allowed us to minister in Millbrook. We returned to Canaan in June of 2000. During this time Canaan was relocating to east Montgomery and embraced the name Sanctuary. We reunited and committed ourselves to continue serving with Pastor Brown in whatever capacity the ministry needed. For the next nine years God would use us in this ministry in many ways, wearing several hats and just enjoying seeing God work.

It was during the season of 2009 that my beloved Vera was diagnosed with dementia. A few years after this diagnosis was made she would step back from serving in ministry. Our children planned a surprise 40-year anniversary for Vera and me. You see, we were married at the pastor's parsonage in Charleston, South Carolina, and never experienced the wedding thrills. Well, they did it for us. I remember Emmett, my son-in-law, blindfolding me as we got into the car. He said with a laugh, "Dad, I was told to do this." So, they drove us around for a while and then helped us out of the car. We entered the Millbrook Civic Center blind-folded where over eighty plus friends and family assembled to celebrate with us. What a thrill that was! It was a joyous occasion. We surely experienced what we did not forty years earlier: cutting of the wedding cake and feeding it to each another, sipping of champagne (sparkling cider), and dancing first to the Temptations song, "It's Growing." Of course, that was our favorite song. This was a glorious, festive time in our lives that we would always remember.

Vera Louise Brown was truly a godly wife, mother, and woman of God. God used her life to impact so many lives. Only eternity would tell of the multitude of souls who have been reached in some way by her life. Her legacy will live on in our hearts. Indeed we should "Just do what God say do." She transitioned and entered God's presence on January 8, 2018 at 11:25 PM. We look forward to the day we will see each other again. I thank her for being the wife, mother, and woman of God she was. God has given her the victory!

Chapter 4

THE JOYFUL HOMEMAKER
By Vera L. Brown

"She opens her mouth with wisdom; and in her tongue is the law of kindness." Proverbs 31:26

"I am the door, if anyone enters by Me, he will be saved, and will go in and out and find pasture. The thief does not come except to steal, and to kill, and to destroy. I have come that they may have life, and that they may have it more abundantly." John 10:9-10

Only Jesus Christ can give us life and when we have new life in Christ we will have the joy of the Lord in our hearts. Joy is one of the fruit of the Spirit. (Galatians 5:22) What is Joy? Joy is knowing that I belong to Jesus, doing His will in my life and living in the role that He has called me to. Joy is knowing that when I should have died for my own sins, Jesus died for me and took my sin and buried them in the deepest sea, never to remember them no more. Joy is John 3:16. So a person must first have joy in their hearts and this joy only comes from knowing Jesus Christ as their personal Savior. Let Jesus give the joy!

Being a homemaker is an art and it is not an easy job, but we have the Lord to give us strength and His Word to give us the know-how. First, we must know what our role is as women and accept it and work and live in that role. We just don't grow into being a homemaker, but it is taught to us by older women: "…that they admonish the younger women to love their husbands, to love their children, to be discreet, chaste, homemakers, good, obedient to their own husbands, that the Word of God may not be blasphemed" (Titus 2:4-5).

> I. Origin of the Home – a woman's role is to be a helpmeet to her husband: And the Lord God said, "It is not good that man should be alone; I will make him a helper comparable to him." "Therefore, a man shall leave his father and mother and be joined to his wife, and they shall become one flesh" (Genesis 2:18, 24). Remembering that the husband is the head of the home: "For I have known him, in order that he may command his children and his household after him, that they keep the way of the Lord, to do righteousness

and justice, that the Lord may bring to Abraham what He has spoken to him" (Genesis 18:19).

II. Center of the Home
    a. Activities and atmosphere of the home should be centered around the husband and children.
    b. What are the responsibilities of a good Homemaker?
        i. Love her husband and children, discreet, chaste keepers at home (Titus 2:4-5)
        ii. Busy and takes care of her own household (Proverbs 31:27)
        iii. Guide the home (1 Timothy 5:14)
        iv. Home builder (Proverbs 14:1)
        v. Diligent (Proverbs 10:4)
        vi. Wise, understanding (Proverbs 24:3-4)
    c. The home reveals the woman. We should have a decent and orderly home, and it should reflect the person of Christ and not a stumbling block to others.

III. The Atmosphere of the Home – We are the key to the atmosphere of the home and our goal and prayer should be that the family will live in peace with one another (Isaiah 32:18) and that the family will live together in unity (Psalm 133:1) and on one accord as one family in Christ. Whatever is done for her family (Proverbs 15:17) should be out of love and not as a sense of duty.

IV. We should look at our Christian homemaking as a ministry to family and to others.
   a. Ministry to her family – These are some principles for ministering to one's family
      i. Our heart attitude must be right, perfect, blameless (Psalm 101:2)
      ii. We must be faithful in all things (1 Timothy 3:11)
      iii. Be a good steward with what God has given you (Luke 16:10)
      iv. Use time wisely (Proverbs 31:27)
   b. Cleaning and housekeeping – What is the purpose?
      i. God wants our home to be peaceable and in order (1 Corinthians 14:33)
      ii. Never know when visitors will come (Luke 19:5-6); receive them joyfully
      iii. To the glory of God (1 Corinthians 10:31)
      iv. To teach our children (Proverbs 22:6)
   c. Practical points
      i. Organize her household so that housework can be done quickly. If you are a working mom, get help.
      ii. Make a schedule for what needs to be done weekly; do most important first
      iii. Make menus for meal planning a week or two at a time

                iv. Allow children to help. Give them responsibilities
            d. A few notes adapted from Letters to Karen:
                i. The good homemaker is organized.
                ii. The good homemaker takes pride in the home but not too casual.
                iii. The good homemaker makes pleasure out of duty.

"Most footprints on the sands of time were made with work shoes."

Prayer: "Help us as homemakers to just do what God say do." V.L.B.

Chapter 5

WOMEN IN THE HOME
BY VERA L. BROWN

"Who can find a virtuous woman? For her price is far above rubies." Proverbs 31:10

"Who can find a virtuous wife? For her worth is far above rubies. The heart of her husband safely trusts her; so he will have no lack of gain…Charm is deceitful and beauty is passing, but a woman who fears the Lord, she shall be praised. Give her of the fruit of her hands, and let her own works praise her in the gates." Proverbs 31:10-11,30-31

This chapter in the book of Proverbs speaks to the life that Vera lived and modeled for others to emulate. The woman's role in the home was something especially

dear to her heart. She emphasized this responsibility and position on numerous occasions. I would like to share a message she gave at conferences regarding the topic "Women in the Home."

The home is the first organization to be founded by God, and it was established by Him in the time of man's innocence. God designed and created man and woman to be different from each other, yet uniquely fitted for the specific tasks He assigned to them. There was no overlapping authority; each had his and her place.

In the bible we read of the tasks for which God made woman: to be a companion to the man, to be a helpmeet for him, and to be a mother of children so that we can replenish the earth as God commanded. The home is the main area of service to God. Genesis 1:28

This ideal woman is described in Proverbs 31 to show what God wants a wife to be and that her home and family are the center of her existence. Men have a different center of service.

In the New Testament the older women are given the responsibility of teaching younger women what God wants them to be. Titus 2:4-5

God is served by a wife when she donates to the cause of God and society a healthy husband who is secure, having all his needs met at home and well adjusted, healthy children who know how to respect themselves and respect the rights of others.

"In the world – But not of it" (John 15:15-16) As long as Christians are living, they will be subjected to the influences of the world, but do not let the world mold you into its mold. We are being swayed by what the world thinks through television, radio, magazines, and motion pictures. However, the Word of God has given us the guidelines on how we should live. When our Lord prayed, he was praying for us that we would be kept from the evil in this world. Sometimes the world makes the Christian homemaker feel that her role is unglamorous and that she is missing all that life has to offer, but remember Christian woman that this is our calling from God and we should be content with what God has called us to do.

"Put away childish things" – (1 Corinthians 13:11) Unfortunately there are married women who are still immature and cannot take on the responsibility of being housewife, mother, lover, and all the other things God wants her to be. But there is help for each of us. We have a loving heavenly Father who is concerned about the details of our lives. Let me now share some points regarding Women in the Home.

1. Her Response to God as a person.
    a. Her love for God first; the greatest commandment is to love God with all thy heart, soul, mind and strength and thy neighbor as thyself – Matthew 22:37-39.
    b. Christ must be Lord of our lives; putting Him first in all areas – Romans 12:1-2.
        i. Prayer life – Philippians 4:6-7; John 15:7
        ii. Share our faith – 1 Peter 3:15; Romans 1:16
        iii. Obedience – Luke 6:46; John 14:21
        iv. Fellowship – Hebrews 10:24-25

- v. Time in the Word – 1 Peter 2:2; 2 Timothy 3:16-17
- c. How is your personal time with the Lord? In order for us to be what Christ would have us to be, we must have a close obedient walk with our Lord and Savior Jesus Christ, putting all of our moods and emotions under His divine control.
2. Her Response to her husband
   a. Her purpose – Genesis 2:18, 24
      i. <u>Helpmeet for man</u> – wife Ephesians 5:22
         1. She is one who satisfies and helps to complete her husband's life. The husband desperately needs her in her role so that he can fulfill his own God given task.
         2. She must recognize and accept her husband's headship and authority.
         3. She listens to and is sensitive to what her husband says and makes mental and or actual notes of his desires.
         4. She is obedient and carries out her husband's desires as soon as possible
      ii. Wife – Ephesians 5:22
         1. To love him, obey, reverence, to be loyal; trustworthy, to honor; be careful concerning finances; bare and care for his children; to be a keeper at home; keep her appearance

iii. Submission – Genesis 3:16; Ephesians 5:22-24, 33; 1 Peter 3:1-2
   1. This is a command from God whether we like it or not. When we refuse, we are being disobedient to God and all disobedience is sin; therefore, we cannot expect the blessings of God on our lives unless we are willing to obey God.
   2. Submission is God's tool for our happiness, and it is not slavery. You can voice your opinion by speaking the truth in love (Ephesians 4:15); one should seek to be submissive to her own husband's desires when he reaches a decision, and that she complies with his requirements whenever possible.
iv. Love – Titus 2:4-5; 1 Corinthians 13
   1. We are also commanded to love our husband and not try to change him or mold him into the image that we want. Love is kind! Are we kind and do we treat our husbands with common courtesy? Love shows approval. We should express approval of our husband, not only in private but also in public.
v. Pray – 1 Thessalonians 5:17
   1. We are commanded to pray one for another, so we should always pray for our husbands. Always remember to pray for his

special needs, job, and the ministry that he is involved in.
    vi. Fulfill his sexual desires – 1 Corinthians 7:4-5
        1. Sex is as much an integral part of marriage as a man and a woman. If one partner has not accepted his or her sexual role in the marriage relationship the mate is driven to find other means of satisfying his or her need. Satan uses this to bring about various sexual and moral defeats in lives that God would otherwise use, and Christ is thereby dishonored.
3. Her response as a mother
   a. Love – Proverbs 31:26-29; Ephesians 6:4
      i. Children need to feel wanted, loved, and an important part of the family. Children also sense a lack of love and acceptance when parents give them things instead of themselves. No child is spoiled by love; a child is spoiled by indulgence.
   b. Teaching or Training Center– Deuteronomy 6:6-7
      i. We must teach our children by example and word; whereas a father is responsible for the spiritual well-being of his family, but we as mothers must carry on the absences of the father. A mother can read the children bible stories, have prayer with them, and show them God's love throughout the day. She can show them in the

midst of their arguments, injuries, and misplaced articles, His instructions to them and how to find God's will in any situation.

4. Her response to her home – being a homemaker is not an easy job, but we have the Lord to give us the knowledge how to do the job. We must know what our roles are as women and accept it and work and live in that role. We just do not grow into being a homemaker, but it is taught to us by older women.
   a. What are the responsibilities of a good homemaker?
      i. Love her husband, children and be discreet chaste keepers at home. Titus 2:4-5
      ii. Busy and takes care of her own household – Proverbs 31:27
      iii. Guide the home – 1 Timothy 5:14
      iv. Homebuilders – Proverbs 14:1
      v. Diligent – Proverbs 10:1
      vi. Wise and understanding – Proverbs 24:3-4
   b. The home reveals the woman. We should have a decent and orderly home and it should reflect the person of Christ and not be a stumbling block to others.
   c. We should look at our Christian homemaking as a ministry to family and others.
   d. Cleaning and housekeeping – what is the purpose?
      i. God wants our home to be peaceable and in order – 1 Corinthians 14:33

      ii. Never know when visitors will come – Luke 19:5-6
      iii. To the glory of God – 1 Corinthians 10:31
5. Six Keys to a Happy Marriage
    a. Maturity
    b. Submission
    c. Love
    d. Communication
    e. Prayer
    f. Christ
6. Five of the common problems of mental adjustments in a marriage
    a. Finances
    b. Social life
    c. Family
    d. Appearance
    e. Courtesy

I hope these principles give one insight on the role of women in the home. May God bless you and remember to: *"Just Do What God Says!"*

Chapter 6

Remembering and Honoring Mom

"Her children rise up, and call her blessed; her husband also, and he praises her." Proverbs 31:28

Her children rise up and call her blessed.
Proverbs 31: 28a

Mel's Memoires of Mom

Where do I begin? Sitting here today preparing my heart to write about Mom is surreal. It just seemed like yesterday that she slipped away from all of us. My heart misses her deeply. There have been so many times I have tried to sit and calculate my thoughts to write this memoire about Mom, but the words did not come easy. Where do I start? There are so many memories, so many life lessons, so much I have learned, and so much to say about, my mother, Vera L. Brown. No matter of time within months could be enough to gather what I would like to say to honor my mom. First and foremost, words cannot even express and would not even be enough to say how thankful and grateful I am to have had a mother like her.

> Give her of the fruit of her hands, and let her own works praise her in the gates. Proverbs 31:31

As I reminisce, there are times where I could still hear her hearty laugh and her signature "hello" when she answered the phone. Her hellos were so welcoming and a solace for me especially when my family was away in Germany or stationed far away. It seemed like she was always there to lend the ear and the advice I needed in all of the stations in my life. I learned so much from Mom. She was a Godly, Christian, Proverbs 31 Woman and wife, who wore a million hats and kept our family together. Mom was always there. I do not remember a time when Mom was out of reach. Her presence graced our home, from the time we got up in the morning until the time my siblings and I came home from school. Mom shared so much love to us. She encouraged each and every one of us to be who God has called us to be without reservation.

Fond memories of holidays, especially Thanksgiving and Christmas, still resonate within me. Mom, you were the center of making the holidays special with all of your signature dishes, recipes, and décor that dressed each room in our home. I still see the laced tablecloths, the china, that sweet smell of spiced tea, the carrot cake, the simmering potpourri in the living room, the kumquats and the variety of nuts sitting on the living room table. You were always setting the tone for a peaceful and welcoming home. I do not take anything for granted. I keep these fond memories close and have been bringing them into my own family life.

When I think about my gifts, talents, and skills, I think of how much Mom had a part of cultivating them. I am the woman I am today because of her imprint on the way I dress, the way I handle the things in my home, to the way I carry myself.

Mom, I see your fingerprints in my life everywhere I look around me. I see you in my own womanhood, my sisterhood, my humanity, and how to be a great and true friend to others. You taught me how to serve, to live in confidence and humility. You showed me how to mind what matters and to always put God first. You modeled worshipping God in many areas of my life and what it should look like, in my home, with my talents, in my ministry, and with my time. I have learned elegance, cultivating a home, and hospitality by your emulation.

Strength and dignity? Mom always encouraged me to appreciate who God created me to be, the way He designed and crafted me, without apology and to always be strong even when I encountered the valleys of life.

> Who can find a virtuous woman? For her price is
> far above rubies Proverbs 31: 10

Dear Mom (Vera B),

Thank you, Mom, for being there through my younger years of sharpening my piano, songwriting, and musicianship skills, putting me into tap classes, taking the time to show me how to cook, going to my recitals, coming to my sports games, school programs, helping me learn how to sew and to be creative, preparing me for college and how to excel in life. You were there when I got married, you were there when I had my children, and you blessed them. You were there to answer questions when I moved into various stages of womanhood. Thank you for your rich deposit. Thank you for being there!

I love you and miss you dearly. I want you to know that your special touch and the unforgettable memories that you have deposited within me will always be stored in my heart, and I will do everything within the power that God has downloaded into me to continue on with your legacy of "Doing what God says do".

Carmela E. Head

Remembering My Mom

As I reflect on my mother, Vera Louise Brown, what better foundation to share who she was than with the meaning of her name. The name, Vera, means "faith" and "truth," and the name, Louise, means "renowned warrior." These are the perfect words to describe who she was and still is to me.

Faith

> "I have been crucified with Christ. It is no longer I who live, but Christ who lives in me. And the life I now live in the flesh I live by **faith** in the Son of God, who loved me and gave himself for me." Galatians 2:20

Mom loved the Lord with all her heart and with such deep passion. She read Scriptures and held personal devotions daily. I remember many days seeing her seated reading her bible or listening to sermons on the radio while she cooked breakfast or washed a load of clothes. In the midst of all the busyness and needs of each day, she kept Christ first and fostered her relationship with Him. She loved Him to the fullest, and it overflowed into all the facets of her life: Her marriage, her family, her home, her friendships, her travels, her ministry, and even her hobbies. Mom believed in keeping a clean home, and one of her favorite hobbies was decorating it. She adorned her dining room table with beautiful settings, displayed pictures of those she held near and dear throughout the house, and could never have enough sheer curtains draping her windows, pillows covering her couch, or doilies on her end tables. It was definitely Vera's touch in every room. She wanted her home to be inviting and used it as an opportunity to welcome others to her home to minister to them and show them the love of Christ. She also loved writing letters. She had such beautiful penmanship. She would leave a note with a bible verse and a word of love or motivation to help you through your day. When I moved away for college, she wrote me letters often. She began her letters with "Praise the Lord for He is good to all," and ended them with "May the Lord bless and keep you." I looked forward to receiving her letters because every letter she wrote always flowed with Scripture to encourage me and point me to the Lord.

She was a woman of faithful prayer regardless of the circumstances. Her trust and dependence were in the Lord to cover her and her family, to meet every need, and to lead and guide her for His work. I have fond memories of her praying with me at my bedside at night and praying with me and my brother before we would leave for school. She also would encourage me to be a woman of prayer, to pray when things are great and when things are challenging. She pushed me to pray for guidance and direction for my own life and to be transparent with the Lord because He is my Heavenly Father. She reminded me that He cares for me, and He cares about the things that concern me. I am truly thankful for her showing me how critical prayer is in my Christian walk.

She desired for others to experience the same joy and freedom she had in Christ. She longed to see others come to know Him and to grow in their walk with the Lord, and so she served. She served as a bible camp counselor, Sunday school teacher, storyteller, devotional leader, conference speaker, and marriage workshop facilitator. She was committed to her convictions with layers of passion, strength, dignity, and love. So, whether she spoke before a group, evangelized door-to-door, held a one-on-one private conversation, or discipled others through life experiences, she kept her mission the same: to sow a seed or water a seed and trust the Lord for the increase.

Truth

> "God is spirit, and those who worship him must worship in spirit and **truth**." John 4:24

Mom was the real deal. I smile as I think about how transparent and honest she was. She cared for those she loved, and it showed with her dedication, support, and loving heart. She showed me what it meant to be a loving, devoted wife. She modeled how marriage was teamwork, husband and wife going through life together to fulfill the ministry the Lord placed on their union. She covered her husband in prayer and walked with him to bring to fruition the vision he saw for his family. She traveled many miles by military and ministry with him and saw the vision unfold. She prayed diligently for him while he served miles away from home in the military. She stood beside him through the founding of two churches. She ministered with him through marriage counseling and leadership conferences, sharing with others the foundational truths for marriage and family. She supported his endeavors as he pursued his degrees in ministry and wrote his book on marriage and family. She was there being the powerful pillar of strength and encouragement. Of course, there were challenges, but she demonstrated how grace and commitment help you through those days. They truly were partners and enjoyed life together. I can reflect on many memories and look back at countless pictures and remember that their smiles and laughter were genuine. They were such a great team.

Mom was the real deal. She stepped away from her career to fulfill her calling as a mother in the home. She was present in my life and in the life of my siblings. She cooked delicious meals, reminiscent of Charleston and made sure we ate together at the dinner table. She taught us how to take care of ourselves and be independent. She challenged us to be thinkers, to be proud of who we are, and to be hard workers. She took time for each of us, talking with us about our daily experiences and listening to our concerns. She made each of us feel special and loved. Birthday parties, long nights of homework, ball games, piano recitals, band performances, presentations, proms, graduations, weddings, she was there. We knew that when we would scan the crowd, she would be there smiling, nodding her head, clapping, or cheering. She was a faithful support. We could call her anytime and know that she would take time for us. I knew that I could go to her about anything. There were times when I made embarrassing decisions, choices that could have had a major impact on my life. She never made me feel ashamed or allowed me to dwell in life's pity parties. She shed tears with me, was very real with me about my choices, and then pushed me to move forward in my walk with the Lord, to keep my perspective eternal.

Mom was the real deal. She was serious about family and her friends. She loved her siblings with all her heart. It did not matter how far away we lived, she made sure we took time to see family and support one another. When I was a little girl we lived at Whiteman, Air Force Base in Missouri, which was a long way from Charleston, South Carolina, but that did not matter to her. We took a road trip every summer to Charleston to see my aunts, uncles, and cousins. She made sure to hold personal conversations with my cousins, to remind them of the love the Lord had for each of them and to encourage them in their journey. While there she visited with her aunts and uncles as well. It was a wonderful time just enjoying family. She also displayed this same passion for her friendships. She had close friends with whom she would visit, dine, shop, and pray. Friendships were valuable to her, and she treasured them. I have so many memories of Mom with her best friend (my godmother), Nadine. They were always together, talking and laughing and supporting each other while their husbands ministered together. Mom, Aunt Nadine, my god sister (Elita), and I spent countless weekends shopping together, going to church together, and eating at the Chinese restaurant after service. It was always a fun time of fellowship. Those were such sweet, impressionable moments. I did not realize it at the time, but she showed me the importance of cultivating relationships, cherishing friendships, making time for those you love, and showing them how much you care about them.

Renowned Warrior

> "I have fought the **good fight**, I have finished the race, I have kept the faith." 2 Timothy 4:7

Mom was the strongest woman I know. She kept her mind on things eternal and defended her faith in the Lord. She would often say, "Just do what God says." She did just that.

As her location changed, she fervently looked for opportunities to serve, build relationships, and advocate for others. She intentionally got to know her neighbors and the families at her church. She would take time to speak with them or invite them to dinner. She was never a stranger. She actively shared the gospel with children and taught them scriptures and songs about the bible, especially during bible camp season, vacation bible school, and Sunday school. She also had a heart for pastors' wives. She knew the unique experiences and emotions of women who held this position. She ensured that they were afforded occasions to engage with other pastors' wives, to receive encouragement, support, and fellowship in order to continue the journey of ministry.

As the culture changed, she stood firm to the scriptures, not allowing herself to be swayed by every wind of doctrine or every passing trend. She modeled before me and my sister attire that was stylish and elegant, remaining appropriate and god-honoring before our brothers in the faith. She enjoyed various styles of music and taught me to appreciate them as well. As I began to make my own musical choices, she would listen with me and challenge me to listen beyond the music to the lyrics and determine how they impacted my life. She taught me how to guard my mind and my heart, to be careful what I allowed myself to hear. She also challenged me to read and know the bible for myself, to not simply go along with what someone says but to return to the scriptures. There were and still are numerous trends in churches that feed the itching ears of the flesh. She taught me not to get caught in them but to remain true to the Word of God and fight for holiness.

As the seasons of life changed, she held on to the wisdom that was instilled in her and continued to move forward in what God said she needed to do. She stood strong for her husband, not allowing anyone to speak or do harm to him. She covered in him prayer daily. She recognized the spiritual battle and knew it was best met in prayer. She fought for her children and remained firm in her nurturing, discipleship, and discipline. She held us accountable and corrected us when necessary. We did not always enjoy those experiences, but I am convinced that as we each reflect, we can express tremendous thanks for her caring about us enough to discipline us when we needed it. She watched us mature into adults and continued to fight for us to stay in the Word and seek the face of the Lord. She not only was our mother, but she became our best friend, rooting for us through each milestone we met. She also remained steadfast in her work for the Lord, even when faced with her illness. She kept teaching. She kept writing. She kept sharing. She kept singing. She kept praising. She fought the good fight, and she fought passionately hard.

My mother, Vera, was amazing, and her life shined so brightly and touched so many. There are not enough words to express how grateful and blessed I am to be her daughter. I would not be the woman, wife, and mother I am today without her. I pray that I can carry on her legacy in my relationship with my daughter. I thank my mother for all the wonderful memories I have of her and for being a woman of faith, standing on the truth, and fighting the good fight through it all.

I love you, Mom.
Renita D. Matthews

FROM A BEST FRIEND TO A BEST FRIEND

DEAR MOM

There is so much I want to say, I don't know where to start,
But I do know you are always there for me,
If I'm home or if we're apart.
Thanks for the long talks we have every day
And for the encouragement you give me as I go my way.
I know there have been times we have shed tears,
We've told each other secrets and shared our deepest fears.
But there was a purpose, for that I am glad to know;
It deepened our friendship and kept us close.
And then we have our arguments that seem to last eternity,
But I know you are just opening my eyes so I can see reality.

So I'll say thanks again for being there until the very end,
For being a great Mother, in other words, my **BEST FRIEND**.

Love Always, Renita (Circa 1995)

REFLECTIONS OF MY MOTHER, VERA L. BROWN
(Momma Brown)

A mother's love is something that I believe no one can accurately comprehend. A mother's love is one that is unbreakable and hard to fathom. It's amazing what a Mother's love can do for her son. I believe that there is nothing outside of God's grand plan for our lives. However, on the ninth day of January 2018, I had the most difficult time understanding God's plan. I still try to make sense of why my mother had to be afflicted with Alzheimer's disease to begin with.

As I sit here and reflect on my mother, I always think of the time in my life when my father was enlisted in the Air Force and we lived at Shaw AFB, South Carolina. I recall us living in base housing on Gardenia street and then moving to 5417-B, Boxwood Circle, which was still located on the base but just on a different side.

When I think of that time frame during my childhood, television shows like Good Times and Little House on the Prairie summed up the feeling that I get deep inside when I think of my Momma Brown (that's what I'd call her). She was always there for me as her presence provided the stress-free environment that I needed, always caring about my well-being.

When I think of Momma Brown, I think of Ephesians 6:1-3 that reads, *Children, obey your parents in the Lord, for this is right. Honor your father and mother – which is the first commandment with a promise – so that it may go well with you and that you may enjoy long life on the earth.* I believe I honored my mother as I loved her so and never wanted to disappoint her. Momma Brown was very instrumental in ensuring that we followed the will of God for our lives. And as her favorite quote states, "Just do what God says to do", that's what I've tried to achieve daily. She taught us the word of God and ensured that we prayed each night. I remember the times she would pray with my brother, Patrick, and me by the bedside each night, instilling a constant prayer life that has stayed with me and my siblings to this very day.

Momma Brown and I would always have constant conversations about life. I remember these conversations that took place from a very young age until I was a grown man. I'd call her often when I was in college and when I became a husband. Gosh, I remember the long phone conversations as if it were yesterday. Seems she always had the answers to my every question. No matter the situation that I may have gone through or which I may have needed her guidance. She took the time to listen and then she'd give her insight regarding that situation. Momma Brown had a way of wise counsel that had to be from God. She was such a woman of God who knew the word and followed the word. And I saw how my friends would also come and talk to her with their concerns. She was not just my mother, but a mother to my friends as well.

Momma Brown had a way with disciplining me that showed me how much she cared. She held me accountable as young boy and continued to hold me accountable when I became a man. She took the time out to teach me how to cook, how to iron, how to sew and how to wash my clothes, iron my clothes and put them away. All these things that she taught, the chores that had to be completed, were what made me the man that I am today. I later understood the importance of keeping my room clean, washing, ironing, and putting my clothes away because when I went off to college, I was able to put into practice all the things I learned from her. I would often stand in amazement at how many young men that I met while living in the college dorm, kept a nasty room, didn't know how to wash clothes, iron their clothes or even fold them. Oh, how I wish she was here even today to see how I keep a clean house and still iron not just my clothes, but my wife's clothes as well, one of the things Vanessa loves about me. Even now though, I would be so thankful to accept Momma Brown's wisdom on situations I face.

Momma Brown had a smile that could soothe any hurt or pains that I may have had. She was such a kindhearted and compassionate woman. When I think of Momma Brown, I also think of Ephesians 4:32, *"Be kind to one another, tender-hearted, forgiving each other, just as God in Christ also has forgiven you.* She taught me how to show compassion. Yet she also showed me how to not be a pushover. One thing about Momma Brown is that she didn't play. She would speak her mind quickly when there was something that she needed to say. And if we happened to step out of line, she'd ensure to get us back on track rather quickly.

Another thing about Momma Brown that I recall is don't mistreat her children. I will never forget the time when we lived on Whiteman AFB, Missouri. My brother, Patrick, and I were walking from one side of the housing area to another side, and we cut through some of the yards. We were almost to our friend's house when a guy came outside and gave us a piece of his mind about us crossing through his yard that wasn't fenced in. Patrick and I were just quickly passing through the yard. We didn't stop, hang out, nor cause any damage to this yard. The names he called us and his tone were not necessary at all. We came home later that day and informed Momma Brown about what transpired. She immediately asked us to take her to this particular residence. She knocked on the door and the man that yelled at us came to the door. He complained about us walking through his yard. Momma Brown quickly put him in check with this fact. She said, "This is the government's property, not yours. My children can walk wherever they please as long as they are not causing any problems". Come to find out, that was my mother's softball coach as she had joined a softball team on the military base that year. If I remember correctly, she also quit the team. This situation showed me that Momma Brown always had our backs and didn't play when it came to her children.

She always instilled in me the drive to not quit. My brother Patrick and I were heavy into sports, and especially baseball. When we were living in Germany, we were on the baseball team called the Wiesbaden Warhawks. We won the youth championship for three years straight. We would travel all over Germany and rest assured that Momma Brown was at every game. I know for certain that she was our biggest fan as I could count on her to be at every game.

I have so many wonderful memories of Momma Brown. It's difficult to put all of my memories down in just a few paragraphs. I am so thankful that I not only had my mother but also my father in our household, which exemplified an example of a nuclear family in where we receive strength and stability from the two-parent structure.

When I think of Momma Brown, this poem sums up my current feelings.

If Roses Grow in Heaven (Dolores M.)

If Roses grow in Heaven Lord please pick a bunch for me.
Place them in my mother's arms and tell her they are from me.
Tell her I love her and miss her, and when she turns to smile
Place a kiss upon her cheek and hold her for a while.
Because remembering her is easy, I do it every day.
But there is an ache within my heart that will never go away.
I love you always and forever, Momma Brown.

Your son, Paul C. Brown Jr.

As I reflect on the impact of my mother's life as she was navigating the debilitating illness of dementia, I begin to reflect on the power of her words. If she could read my words in a letter, they would say the following:

Dear Mom,

I miss you and frequently imagine what you would say in this current season. This weekend captures a moment of healing manifestation in me. I had mental blocks of writing about you in navigating the pain of betrayal from those who didn't recognize who you were to me, to us and to many. Now, the reflective gates are open to flow from the well within. The seeds you planted now bud prophetically with forward advance from reflective revelation.

Years after you made your transition, this weekend I consider your legacy and 'in memoriam,' reflect on your teachable moments.

*Legacy is considered anything handed down from the past, as from an ancestor or predecessor. Legacy is not bound by age or time served.

*Legacy represents your body of work at each stage of your life. Herein is what I have conceived, perceived, and received from you to pass on to others.

MOTHERS IMPART COMMUNICATION

You provided an atmosphere for expressing authenticity, transparency and directive clarity. I always knew where you stood and what you were thinking. What you taught me was "how you got that point." And to communicate it with a certain tune and tone whereas not to lose my voice in the noise. As a result, I articulated my positions and thoughts with accuracy and clarity without fear of retaliation and retribution. I learned the responsibility and accountability for my words.

MOTHERS IMPART CRITICAL AND CREATIVE THINKING

I'm reminded of how many questions you asked me. One day as I left you didn't say to be home a certain time. No curfew. In fact you asked me, "So Pat, what time will you be home tonight?" Eh... I had to answer based on my CHARACTER and CREDIBILITY thus your approach to questions caused me to consider WHAT I was doing, WHY I was doing it and WHO was I with—little did I know you were causing me to think before I acted, to explain my thoughts and retain my reasoning. I got "IT" as I grew. Thank you. My life was preserved through those hard questions. Perhaps, even saved on a few occasions. I often wonder what decisions could have been made without those challenges.

MOTHERS IMPART COMPETENCIES

As I faced opposition in some educational scenarios, you asked me another question, "Who gave you what is inside of you?" I failed to see the question's relevance at the time based on how I was feeling due to external resistance that eventually built internal resilience. The lesson was one in knowing my competencies and the outcome was that "true hospitality not only loves the gift of God in the human vessel but loves the human which houses the gift." You then shared that they are treating you that way out of NOT knowing who they are, because if they knew who they are they would know HOW to treat you. I learned to be hospitable in spite of how others treat me. To be mindful. To be careful. To be daring enough to show grit, resilience and mental toughness in the face of opposition or while standing alone, to not pursue the herd mentality or submit to overbearing group think.

As I continue to establish legacy for my daughters and impact others with my own words, I would share my lessons from my mother with other mothers.

To MOTHERS, know that your sons hear you even when it seems like they don't.

To those in GRIEF, you can navigate the waters with grace and self-compassion. There may not be the dynamics of replacement but the dynamism of reflection.

Patrick J. Brown

Memory Of My Mother

Mom meant so much to me through the years. Even though I still miss her to this very day. And it is still hard.

I was the fifth and last child she had. She held me in her arms. She was there for me. She took care of me. She looked after me, and she provided for me. She taught me a whole lot of stuff while I was growing up. We would always laugh and play.

I remember she would drive me to school and picked me up from school, and she would take me to the playground. She would also take me shopping and buy me clothes.

She taught me about the bible. She also taught me how to pray and how to love others. She taught me how to stay focused on God and let God guide me and watch over me.

We had our ups and downs. We had fun and had a lot of good times together.

David K. Brown

My Reflections

The first time I met Vera Brown, what I immediately noticed was her smile. It could light up the room and was contagious enough to make anyone give a big cheesing, teeth showing smile back in return, even me which is no easy task. But this shouldn't have been surprising to me, because it was the same thing that initially attracted me to her daughter, Renita. Over the years as I got to know her better, I learned that there was so much more to Mom than a pretty smile. Whether it was from the praises spoken of her from her children, listening to her wisdom, or watching her life, there were so many important lessons that she taught me.

Through her life I learned that she valued relationships, with her husband, her children, her family, and her friends, but none more important than her relationship with Christ. And that spilled over into her relationships with others. You could see it in how supportive she was of her husband whether it was the multiple moves across the country and overseas to Germany during his military service or partnering with him in various ministries through the years. You could see it in the way that she invested in her children. Renita would always tell me how her mom would be at every performance, game, or recital, and not just for Renita, but for all five of Mom's children. You could see it in the closeness she had with her own brother and sisters and extended family. She always made sure that her family made trips back home to South Carolina for reunions, holidays, and visits.

I also learned that she was a worshipper. I often remember her humming a praise song as she cooked or straightened things up around the house. Even as her illness progressed, you'd still hear her singing or humming.

I also learned that she was a prayer warrior. If you ask some people to pray for you, they may tell you that they will, but I always knew that I could count on her prayers. I remember early on when Renita and I were dating, we would leave campus and spend some Sundays at her parents' house. During dinner Mom always asked about my family. Once I shared some troubles my younger brother was dealing with. She sensed my concern and said she would pray for him. Years went by, and she always asked about him, how he was doing, and told me that she was still praying for him.

There are so many more things I could share, but the greatest lesson I learned from Mom came when her illness had progressed to the point that she didn't always recognize us, and she wasn't able to communicate with us. It was during one of the family reunions. We were having a family church service before everyone got on the road to go home. Praise was high, and I remember we had broken into a time of prayer. During this season in our marriage, we had been trying to get pregnant for years, and it just felt like God wasn't going to ever answer our prayer. As everyone else around the church were praying aloud to God, I remember feeling really broken at that time and not understanding why things weren't happening for us. Honestly, I was losing hope. Mom was sitting on the pew behind me. All of a sudden, I felt her hand firmly grip the back of my head, and she began to speak over our marriage, and she boldly proclaimed "Sam, God is going to answer our prayers and bless you and Renita with a child. He will give you the desires of your heart!" As we came out of the prayer time, mom returned to her previous state, and her memory would fade again, but in that moment, I learned to not give up and to hold on. And I also learned that even though her outward body was fading, inwardly she was being renewed daily and fully capable of being used of God.

About three months before the Lord gave Mom her rest, He made good on what Mom spoke over me that day. He answered our prayer and blessed us with our daughter Semeia Vera, Mom's namesake and legacy. We see so much of her spirit in Semeia. I am truly thankful for the life of Vera Brown and the wisdom I gained from knowing her. Renita and I will try our best to foster that same fire and passion within Semeia and teach her those lessons we learned from Mom's legacy.

Samuel Matthews, Jr., Son-in-law

Chapter 7

One, Two, Three into God's Presence

> "Precious in the sight of the Lord is the death of His saints." Psalms 116:15

I decided to take Vera to Charleston for Christmas. It would be great to spend the holidays with family. I did not know it would be our last trip together. Yet, God knew. I was asked earlier to participate in the Motown Review sponsored by the Burke High School Foundation. By the time I responded they had already finalized the various entries. I had planned to bring Vera to the stage and sing a song to her. However, it was not to be since they had all the acts they planned to present. Yet, we attended the program with Joe, Joy, Yolanda, and Adrian. My classmate, Theron, was MC that evening. I thought for a moment to slip him twenty dollars to get on the program, but I did not. It was a wonderful show. Several times I had to help Vera sit up as she was sliding down in her seat. After the show ended, we made our way to the car, making certain that Vera was comfortable and buckled up.

Returning to the house I made preparation for us to go to bed. Vera seemed a bit agitated. She wrestled trying to sleep. Getting up in the morning I made certain she was freshened up and dressed for the day. During breakfast she struggled to eat. Joy took some time to feed her, but she appeared to not want to swallow anything. I supposed it was being away from home and she would do alright when we returned to Millbrook. We prepared to leave; we thanked Joe and Joy for the visit and hugged them. On our travel we made several stops along the way. She ate very little as we traveled. I supposed being away from familiar things affected her appetite. I was certain once we got home, she would eat more.

As the rest of the week evolved her appetite began to decrease as she struggled with swallowing. I contacted her nurse to give her an update on things. The nurse came over and suggested a few things we could do to see if Vera would swallow: soft foods, Ensure, and breakfast drinks. We tried all these, and it was a struggle for her. The nurse told me my greatest fear that we were nearing the end, and I may want to call for the children to come home.

We did attend church with Renita and her husband, Sam, to dedicate Semeia, our granddaughter. Sam's family was present for this special occasion. Vera struggled during the service. I had to assist her with sitting upward. Pastor Cockrell, head of the church, came over to say a special prayer over her. For that I was so thankful as he encouraged us. Semeia was dedicated. Sam and Renita gave her the middle name of Vera, just as Vera and I gave Renita the middle name of Dorothy after Vera's mother. We stopped by a restaurant after church services, but Vera did not eat anything, and she drank very little.

Upon returning home I contacted the nurse who explained what I needed to do during the week. This would be an extremely challenging time for me as I saw my wife declining day by day. It seemed to be at a much faster pace. The children and I agreed a long time earlier that if Vera got to the point of not swallowing, we would not intervene with a feeding tube. I observed the love of my life drifting away. By Sunday, all the kids, except for Paul Jr., were present. Sunday was the last time she was up. It was always a joy for me to get her up, give her a bath, get her dressed, tend to her needs, and make certain her clothes and jewelry matched. This would not be the case as she laid there in the bed. Monday morning Tameka Roper, home help nurse, came by and gave Vera a bath in the bed and changed her pajamas. I was feeling rather weak at this point. There was very little response from Vera. Around noon time I got up in the bed, cuddled up next to her, and sang our three favorite songs: "It's Growing," "Still I will Trust You," and "Through the Years." As I sang tears begin to flow down my face, yet I wanted her to hear me one more time. I recalled so many times before that we would dance and swing to those songs. Music was special to the both of us. We would sing, dance, and enjoy ourselves. There was always music in the house.

The children gathered around her bedside, and each one told their Mom how much they loved her and how much she meant to them. She poured herself into our children, and now God was about to take her home. We kept her comfortable. I was sitting in the chair, and I noticed her breathing became rather rapid. I called the on-call nurse, and she explained that is to be expected.

As the evening approached her breathing became slower. I perceived that time was drawing near as Vera would soon leave us. The children were around her bedside. I was sitting next to her on the bed, kissing her, rubbing her forehead, doing what I could to make her more comfortable, and telling her how much I love her. As the evening drew late her breathing got slower and more labored. Soon after 11:00pm on January 8, 2018, Vera took her last breath and entered into the presence of God. I cannot explain it. Even though

I shed tears as my wife of 49 years just went into eternity, God gave me a peace to see that Vera's struggle was now over.

I thank God for the victory and told the children, "Mom has entered into the presence of Jesus." I called the hospice nurse who came over to confirm Vera's passing. I coordinated with the coroner and notified the funeral home personnel who came to take Vera's body. We stayed in the living room while they prepared to take her out of the bedroom.

As we were left to embrace and encourage one another I had a sense of loneliness. This is permanent, and we would not see her again on this side of heaven. Sleep would escape me. The children were very concerned about me to make certain that I was alright. I began to look around the room, so many memories. Vera and I spent the last 25 years in this house, this room, and now I was left with such good memories. Our family was left to reflect on her life. Even now as I write this chapter I still tear up and sigh. But God! I recall a Mother of Memorial Baptist Church sharing with me that "God knew of this season before you did." Thus, now this time was ordained of God. This would be a night to remember.

Journal Entry

Wednesday January 17, 2018: Today has been one filled with emotions as I reflect on Vera's celebration services on yesterday. The closing of the casket was very hard as it was the last time I would see her physical body. Yet, I know she is in the presence of

God, totally healed. She entered God's presence on January 8, 2018 at 11:20 PM! It has been one week and 2 days, and I miss her so much. I tear up often as I think about her. I find it very strange and cannot explain this empty feeling. Her physical presence is no longer here. I cannot hug her, pull her up, and kiss her. As I reflect on my wife and partner of 49 years, I thank God for all the sweet memories. Praising Him for what He allowed us to accomplish and sow into the kingdom together. Vera Louise Brown, I praise God for you and miss you so very much. I trust to honor your memory. I pray to complete another book and hope to entitle it "Keep Pressing" or "Just Do What God Says." Thank you for allowing me to be your husband. Thank you for five godly children. I love you, Vera, and look forward to seeing you in heaven! Lord, I thank you for this day after.

Chapter 8

TREASURED MEMORIES

Resolution of Respect in Loving Memory of
Vera Louise Brown

Dearest Vera, though your days among us were too brief and our grief at your loss is never-ending, we draw comfort from the knowledge that you have found safe refuge in the Lord and in our hearts, where no darkness or pain can touch you now. We bless you with love, light, and our gratitude.

When Vera went home to be with the Jesus, early Tuesday morning, January 9, 2018, there passed from the walks of life one of the greatest Christians The Sanctuary Church Family has ever had the privilege of knowing. We count it a genuine blessing to have had the opportunity to be a part of her life for over twenty-five years. Her Christian example, her sincerity in ministry, and her passion for marriage and family left indelible marks that are forever etched in our hearts and memory.

Whereas, in the providence of God, He has brought to a close the life of our beloved Vera, the officers and members of The Sanctuary, Historically Canaan Hill Missionary Baptist Church, Montgomery, Alabama, desire to place on record our love and esteem for Vera's life and labor of love, and our deepest sympathy to the family; and

Whereas, the death of Vera does not diminish the profound benediction of a life lived in such Godly service, nor our admiration of and affection for her example, as Vera faithfully attended God's most urgent admonition to follow in the footsteps of the righteous, tend to her family in an unmatched, priceless manner, seek justice in all circumstances, and care for the least among us as if they were the dearest; and

Whereas, Vera was an active member of The Sanctuary for many years and freely gave of her time and energy as a lay leader and faithful member of the congregation—spearheading Children's Church; teaching children's Sunday school, bible study, and Vacation Bible School; serving as a missionary and an evangelist as a door-to-door witness to the community; mentoring our young women while serving as their chaplain; setting an example as a prayer warrior and a worship and devotional leader, all while working cheerfully and tirelessly for over 45 years to reach, teach and train young people via SPOLIWA Ministries; and

Whereas, our beloved Vera shared her bright light, steady spirit, and cheerful heart to all whom she encountered, and embraced the all-forgiving presence of God from earliest days—striving to exhibit these same qualities of compassion throughout an exemplary life for her children to follow—the family and acquaintances of Vera are deeply saddened at her departure, as are all who were touched by her generous spirit and kindnesses. Vera's legacy of faith and service will continue to inspire loved ones and every member of The Sanctuary;

Whereas, be it resolved, therefore, that we bow in humble submission to the will of our Heavenly Father who does all things well, and that we rest in the knowledge that one day we will be reunited with Vera in the joy and fullness of God's mercy. We extend to her family our deepest sympathy, thanking the Lord for the privilege of having known and loved this dear woman;

Whereas, be it also resolved that we will forever cherish her memory and strive to emulate her admirable Christian traits as we also strive, in her words to "do what God says do." May this tribute of respect bear some comfort to the immediate family, other relatives, and friends of Vera; and, to all whom this presence, let it be known that a copy of this resolution will be placed in the historical records of The Sanctuary, Historically Canaan Hill Missionary Baptist Church, and a copy given to the family.

Humbly Submitted on this Sixteenth Day of January, Two Thousand Eighteen, in Faith, Appreciation, and Love for the Gift of Our Time with

Vera Louise Brown.

The Sanctuary
Rev. Ossie T. Brown, Jr.
Senior Pastor

Her children arise and call her blessed; her husband also, and he praises her: "Many women do noble things, but you surpass them all." Charm is deceptive, and beauty is fleeting; but a woman who fears the LORD is to be praised. Honor her for all that her hands have done, and let her works bring her praise at the city gate. Proverbs 31:28-31, NIV

My Dear Friend

I thank GOD for the precious memories of my dear friend, Vera. I was a young divorcee with two children when I met her. I had just given my life to JESUS, but I didn't have any born again Christian friends. I had a lot of good, caring, and moral friends but none that knew and loved JESUS in this new way that I loved Him after I gave Him my heart. As I was excited about CHRIST and tried to talk to them, they thought I was losing my mind. I shared this with the young lady who led me to CHRIST. She went on a mission to find me Christian friends so I could grow in CHRIST. She located someone who gave her Paul Brown's name. He called me at work, invited me to his home. This was my first encounter with Vera Brown, the mighty woman of God who would be my spiritual teacher, spiritual mentor, and my dear friend.

Vera invited me to a women's bible study that she held in her home. This was the beginning of a wonderful relationship. I went to the bible study for several years. It was the source of my early growth in CHRIST. It established my walk with CHRIST. She was an amazing teacher and a compassionate person. She took me under her wings. Not only did she minister to me during bible study, but she had me over constantly along with my children.

Vera was my first teacher of the gospel. She was very instrumental in my becoming the woman of God I am today. I am so grateful that the bible study ended up as a church, New Life Bible Church, where her husband, Paul Brown served as the minister. Vera set a fine example of being a servant in the church. She worked day and night along with her husband in the work of the ministry. Vera was a wonderful wife, mother, and friend.

The one thing that I remember most about Vera was her great love for JESUS. She loved her husband, her children, her family, and her friends, but nothing compared to her love for JESUS! He was truly first in her life. You could see it in her beautiful smile and her eyes. The beauty of the LORD was shown in precious Vera. I could go on and on about this wonderful woman of God, but I will end it here. Vera is in heaven enjoying Jesus, the one for whom she loved and lived her life.

Trusting GOD turns Problems into Opportunities. Love, Loraine Montgomery

I Will See Her Again

When I think of the goodness of the Lord, my soul cried out for saving me. I met Vera at a bible study. She led the study. Vera spoke with a voice of seriousness, "Let's do this," and, "We need to forsake that." She made me feel that whatever the bible said it was for all. I visited St. James, where we met sometimes, and as I sat there, I could hear her voice and see her smile. I will see her when I get home.

Anna Davis

Reflection

My name is Haywood Edmonds, and my wife's name is Maggie L. Edmonds. We met Vera Brown December 1979 in Sumter, South Carolina at Shaw Air Force Base. My wife, Maggie, met Vera Brown on base at an exercise class. Vera, being the type of person she was, asked Maggie to come to church with her. We came to church with her (New Life Bible Church) around December 1979 or January 1980. Vera was the very reason Maggie and I joined New Life Bible Church. She encouraged us to study the bible and be the best husband and wife we could be to each other and our children. Maggie and I had just gotten married in August 1979. She was the virtuous woman according to Proverbs 31 that my wife and I had ever known. She took time with Maggie and me to help us grow as believers in Christ.

Vera loved her family, and it was just what we needed to see to help our marriage. She was a soul-winner, a family person, and a visionary. I will really miss the times we spent talking and sharing things about each other's families. We spent three years at Shaw

Air Force Base (from December 1979 to November 1982). Vera was one of the main reasons our tour at Shaw was a pleasant one. Vera and her family went to Germany. Then Maggie and I went to Germany (from 1982-1985). Vera and her family have been a part of our family since December 1979 until the Lord took her to glory in January 2018. If I had to sum her life up from the time we met until God took her to glory, it would be that: "She was a loving, caring, compassionate, and virtuous woman."

Brother Haywood Edmonds

Treasured memories of my dear Sister Vera Brown

Vera will always be remembered by me for setting a good example of what a real Christian should be. She helped me quite a bit, years ago by taking my children with her and her family to church and Sunday school. When it was time for bible camp, my children were invited too and they enjoyed that. As a result of her caring, listening and most of all her love, I accepted the Lord. She prayed with me and invited me to church too. She read a devotional book by Uncle Charlie from the Children's Bible Hour to our children. The kids really enjoyed it and learned a lot. She was a great storyteller.

I remember Vera taking my children with her and her children to the swimming pool on base in Sumter, South Carolina, and they enjoyed that they were taking swimming lessons at that time. Vera used to like to sew, and I did too. She helped me again to get a pattern put on the material to make something for one of my girls.

I had some health issues one time, and she came to our house on Boxwood Circle in Sumter, South Carolina and helped me with my personal care. She had a busy schedule with her children and her husband, but always gave of herself to help others. I love you, Vera, and am looking forward to hearing you sing and talk to me again. Keep smiling.

Elaine Burnett

From A Neighbor

Dear Paul,

Thank you for asking me to write about Vera. I have tried to remember specific moments I had with her. Since I worked a lot those first years that we were neighbors, I recall more about the later years.

Those first years, I remembered Vera as the kind Christian neighbor. She took care of her family and always had a big smile.

Vera supported her husband and cared for the home front. We spent time sharing our families' news and waving as we went about our busy lives, but I always knew Vera was just next door if I ever needed her.

Vera enjoyed the swing in the backyard and flowers. She spent time planting flowers along the patio and at the front door. As time passed and Vera's illness took more of her, she would stand at her front door and sing. All the time watching over my granddaughter as Ella rode her bike. Vera would always "supervise" Paul's yardwork. Sometimes she would sit in the swing and nap or sing. Occasionally, Vera would walk in the yard "checking out" Paul's work.

I miss the comfort of knowing Vera was just next door. I miss her heart-warming smile and singing as I work in the yard. I miss my neighbor! Sincerely,

Gloria B. Walters

Galatians 6:9-10, tells us to not be weary of doing good for we will reap in due season if we do not give up. So then, we are to do good to everyone especially to those who are of the household of faith. Our dearly departed Sister Vera Brown was not only a hearer of God's Word. She lived the words of these scriptures. She exemplified characteristics of Jesus by being compassionate, loving,

encouraging, hospitable, giving, and friendly. She was a faithful, godly woman yoked to a godly man in one flesh.

Love,
Ernest & Pamela Robinson

My Treasured Memory with Vera

As I think of Vera, my mind often goes back to our conversations. Vera and I could stay on the phone for an hour or more talking. She was an extremely passionate person when it came to the things she believed. I vividly remember a lengthy conversation with Vera as she counseled me about my future role as a husband. I can still hear her words, "Nate, you must learn to listen to your wife. She will need to talk, and you will need to listen without interrupting her. She needs to know that you care about the things she cares about, even if no one else does."

Vera continued, "Paul listens to me, and even at times when I think he has fallen asleep, when I call his name, he responds to my questions and discusses my concerns, so I know he was listening all the time; that means a lot to me."

She would remind me of the things that a husband should do for and with his wife. She would remind me that it is important to spend quality together, not necessarily expensive outings, but quality. This was special to me because it was long before I ever had a wife or was dating anyone seriously. Over the years, these conversations, and many others like them, became very special to me because, although I was not her biological son, she loved me as if I were, and she wanted me to have a good marriage and a good life. I think I loved Vera most for her investment of time in my life. She had a lot of wisdom when it came to rearing children and what they needed to be successful. Not only did she teach me about life and living, but she also celebrated my accomplishments. She could make me feel like a million dollars, or that I had just discovered the cure for cancer. Her positive words of encouragement, her tenacity, and her very generous heart will always bring a smile to my face whenever I think of her. As her testimony was, mine is, "Just do what the Lord says," John 2:5.

Dr. Nate Brock

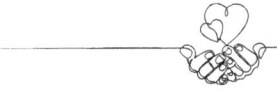

My Sis-in-Law, Vera Brown, was a Christian Woman, who served the Lord with her heart, mind, and soul. God gave her the wisdom and strength to be sustainable in life's endeavors. Vera led her Christian home with integrity and discipline, teaching her children to believe in the Lord Jesus Christ.

I love and admired Vera, because she always gave to me a word of encouragement, such as, "Remain in Christ Jesus," "Stand on the

Word of God," and, "Believe in moving forward in life, conquering life's hurdles." Her virtuous life will remain with me forever.

Sadie B. Green, Sister-in-Law

Sweet Memories of Vera

I can't even remember how or when my relationship/friendship with Vera began. It just happened. We mutually gravitated towards each other at Canaan Hill (now Sanctuary) Baptist Church, and it was as if we had known each other all of our lives. Now, nearly 30 years later, though temporarily separated by her passing, I still find myself thinking about our times together—the lessons she so lovingly taught me without my even knowing it, the advice she gave, the example she displayed, the words she spoke. I was drawn to her "Christian feistiness," for we were both very passionate about "right is right, and wrong is wrong!" As I said at her Homegoing Celebration, Vera taught me how to "fight godly." I don't know if I learned the lessons well, but she was an expert teacher! (Lol!)

Vera and I were not daily or even weekly phone buddies or visiting friends, but when we did call, visit, or travel together, it was nonstop talking, laughing, and fun! Even on Sundays after church, we would talk and talk and talk, and Paul would not interrupt. He would just wait patiently until we were done, asking, "Did y'all get it all out?"

Although memory and speech loss would eventually prevail during her illness, Vera's long-term memory would sometimes kick in. On Sundays, we sat together, but one Sunday, she sat with her children who were visiting. As I turned to greet her and them, she looked at me, pointed her finger, and said, "That's my friend!" I was so moved by her expression! It brought me to tears, and still does. I will always, always cherish our friendship; I miss her dearly.

Pamela G. Brown

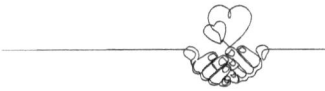

My Big Sister, Vera, meant the world to me. Vera was more than an older sister, she was like a mother. While growing up as children, my siblings and I played house, and Vera was always my mother. As we matured, we grew to be very close with fond memories of our close family bond. Our mother passed away when Joyce and I were 17 years old. As I reflect on life after our mother's passing, I realize that my sister, Vera, became the voice in our lives that spoke wisdom to us as women, provided support when we needed it, and nurtured with spiritual wisdom and direction.

When I gave birth to my eldest son and mom was no longer with us, Vera came to stay with me for a week to help with the new baby. It was through her time spent with me that inspired me to drive a car and gain more independence. Vera and Paul would visit often, and my home was the place that our family called, "home". My husband and I gave up our bedroom a couple of times for Vera and Paul while visiting. I can recall the day that my sister, Vera, spoke wisdom into me and said, "Never give up your bedroom, no matter who it is. Your bedroom is a sacred place for you and your husband."

There were many conversations and memories that I can recall when I think of Vera. The greatest thing to recall is the fact that she was my Sister in Christ and best friend. I am thankful for the blessing that God gave through our relationship. I grew spiritually and naturally by observing her love for God and her love for others.

Joy Shokes

Memories of Sister Vera

Memories of Sister Vera Brown began in the late eighties. Our families were members of Shiloh Missionary Baptist Church (MBC), Warrensburg, Missouri. This family lived their lives demonstrating what a god-fearing life should be.

Our relationship grew while we attended Shiloh MBC, and Sister Brown was truly an inspiration to be around. She often spoke of how good God was. She took care of her family and was always careful about things being done decent and in order. She was kind, humble, and always a pleasure being around her. Her spiritual attitude was the life lived and spoken about.

We dearly miss her. We will always keep her humble spirit in our hearts. She was an excellent example of how a Christian should live, a true follower of Jesus Christ. We will dearly miss her, an inspiration to all.

Sincerely the Cockrell Family

Dedicated to the Memory of Mrs. Vera Louise Brown

The sweetest client I had the pleasure of taking care of. It was not only my job; taking care of Mrs. Vera was a learning experience. I am thankful in that from day one your family welcomed me with open arms. God puts people in our path for a purpose; some are blessings, and some are lessons. Mrs. Vera, your family is a blessing to me. You are in my thoughts often and in my heart always. I thanked God for the time I had with you. I have pictures and memories of you that I will cherish always. Gone, but never forgotten. Rest in heaven, sweet lady. Also, I would last like to thank Mr. Paul Brown for the opportunity to be a part of Mrs. Vera's legacy! May God bless you continually!

I will always remember: "Do what God says do." Your Daughter in Christ

Elaine Parks

"Remembering My Best Friend"

While sitting here recalling such fantastic memories and putting my thoughts and words together with memories of someone I have loved and cherished for so many wonderful years, though hard to do, I find it comforting as I speak of her. Truly, there were memorable years. We shared things we would share for many years ♥. Our families joined forces in 1975.

In August we received PCS orders to Shaw Air Force Base in Sumter, S.C. Shortly after moving into our home on base, our two outgoing daughters, Delfonia and Carmela, brought the Brown and Wingate families together, and we became family as we built a friendship to last forever. This was a blessing in so many ways. I for one really didn't want to go to Sumter, South Carolina, because when I asked others about it, I was like, "What!" Then going with a newborn and a feisty seven-year-old to a place where I knew nobody, was not my most proud moment. But God knew different. As I said earlier, we met the Browns and became family and friends, a friendship that grew into a Christian Lifetime story. At Shaw AFB, we attended church together. Vera taught a Christian Charm class that really brought some lovely ladies and young ladies together to bring the beauty of the hearts and outer beauty to show what God's design of beauty is. That class was just the beginning of Vera's ministry at Shaw AFB. To expansion, she was involved with

SPOLIWA in Warner Robins, GA. She opened her heart, home, and her love for the Lord to EVERYONE she met.

We had days that we spent shopping, laughing, talking, and buying fabric. We made outfits for every weekend. She became not just my friend but my sister, the godmother of our daughter, Elita, and Aunt Vera to all our children. They will cherish that forever.

Shaw Air Force Base was just the beginning when we shared many years there. Even when time came that we had to go to different bases we were always in touch and reaching out to one another, sharing everything that we were doing through many miles and countries. During our time in the military, we were in different states and different countries, but our friendship just grew and grew and blossomed into something that I can't even explain. Our children grew together even with the miles between us.

I have been so blessed to have this lady in my life and even now I can see her smiling and saying things like, "Girl, they better ask somebody." That was one of our favorite sayings. When we were out, we went from Shaw Air Force Base to Virginia to Germany to Alaska to Panama to Germany, so many bases, Missouri, Homestead Air Force Base. You name it, and we had gone there. Yet, we always found our way back to each other, to just sit and talk. Even that was a time to just share. We were teaching classes at the camp and just sharing. She smiled with each person she was around, a gracious woman. Class truly exemplified her because she shared that in her life, with her younger generations, her daughters, my daughters, and so many who came to know her.

We left our PCS station and transferred to Alabama. There was never a break in our friendship or the time that we shared because we kept in touch. My family and I moved into our home, and I began my interior design business. Guess who was there too, along as one of the designing women? Yes, my friend, Vera, and we saw our friend, Vicky Williams, at that time. We took the name of the Designing Fantastic Three. I cannot say how much we enjoyed going out on location and just working together to make another family's home beautiful. This was one of Vera's passions and proudest moments to go in and put her design into someone's heart because your heart was at home.

There are so many wonderful things I can share about my sister and dearest friend, but the truth is you who knew her as knew who she was till her last breath. We know there is one more angel in heaven working in the presence of the Lord. As I'm sharing this, I hear her saying, "If they don't know, they better ask somebody." This was one of our favorite quotes. So, I say that I lost a woman I will FOREVER LOVE & LAUGH ABOUT when I look at her photos with the beautiful smile she always had that would light up so many faces. I am blessed to have had shared so many wonderful memories and years with such "A Gracious and Loving Woman." I will love ya, girl, and miss ya like crazy.

Nadine Wingate

Vera, My Friend, My Buddy

When I read Proverbs 31, I think about my special friend, Vera. To this day, I feel within my heart, the Lord ordered my family's steps to Germany for the sole purpose of "Meeting the Browns". The impact they made on the life of my family is beyond words. But for me it was Vera, who became my buddy/friend, my confidante, my Sister-In-The-Lord, and everything else that I cannot express in words who helped me become the person I am today.

For the life of me I cannot remember when we actually met in Germany, (probably in the evening Gospel service), but we became the bests of friends. Our families began hanging out together, traveling together, and Vera babysat my youngest, Shanita, while I worked. She and I had many conversations about our children and husbands. When my children got on my last nerve, she would always keep me in check or give me little tidbits of her wisdom on how to say things "in a nice way". (Oh, Vera, you just don't know how I miss those talks).

Oh, when I think of all the good times, my heart fills with so much joy! Our families, the Browns, the Parish's, and the Robinsons traveled together a lot, skiing, parks, etc., and we were just one big happy family. We were such a family that one Thanksgiving, Vera suggested to Gloria and me that we celebrate together, and we could have it at my house. I don't know how the word got out to the single soldiers in our service, (Vera), but it did. We had a great time! It was such a gathering of love and fellowship and I remember Vera, Gloria, and I reminiscing after everything was over about God's love flowing from heart to heart.

I remember the time Vera decided to start a ladies' bible study. We would go from house to house and study God's Word. I know for a fact that it was through these studies, Vera helped me grow in the Lord, develop a quiet time devotional routine which helped me to get to know God in a more personal way and make Him Lord of my life, not only me, but the other ladies as well. We became not your typical ladies' bible study group who just came together once a week, hold bible study, and went about our lives to the next week. We became sisters; confiding our fears, our desires, laughing, crying, and encouraging each other as we went through our ups and downs. And we ate a lot! Not only were we feeding our spiritual body, we also fed our physical body. So that was when we decided we needed to work off some pounds. So, we started going to the gym to exercise and take care of our physical bodies.

It was during one of these times when we were relaxing in the sauna in the gym just chit chatting that they had an emergency on the base, and we had to evacuate. Of course, everyone was panicking because we had no idea what was going on, but we knew we had to get dressed in a hurry and get out. One of the sisters became hysterical and started hyperventilating and Vera, being the person she was, stopped getting herself together and took care of the sister. While we were all focused on getting out, Vera talked calmly and dressed the other sister, then herself. My Vera was that caring and loving person, always thinking of others before herself.

Yes, I call her my Vera, my friend, my buddy, because she was there for me when I couldn't help myself. When I got the news from home that my father was dying and they had given him only 48 hours at the most to live and there I was living in Germany, thousands of miles away wanting to get home to my dad, all I could do was cry and call Vera. On the phone, all I did was cry. The next thing I knew, my Vera and a couple more of the ladies came to my house, packed up all my families' clothes, and everything we would need to travel. And Vera physically dressed me and helped my children prepare to go to the airport.

My Vera, my friend, my buddy, my sister who taught me to love tea, who shopped, walked, and laughed with me as we went to the German Christmas marts sampling grilled mushrooms, wurst, and hot chocolate, who sat in the car outside with me for hours and hours talking about family and God, who introduced me to women retreats and led and taught me how to lead souls to Christ. Yes, just as in Proverbs 31:10, if anyone asked me "Who could find a virtuous woman?" my answer will always be my Vera.

Joann Parish

Vera Brown – A Proverb 31 Woman

I was told about Vera months before I met her. We both lived off Elder Drive at Shaw AFB, SC in 1977. A friend of mine was introducing me to the base and pointed out that there was a lady that had 7 or 8 kids. Wow, as military mothers that was a lot. While being in a backslidden state and both my friend and I being abused wives, we laughed our way through our pain. Everything and everybody was funny. One summer, Pastor Paul Brown stopped by my friend's house to invite her son to SPOLIWA Bible Camp in Jeffersonville, Georgia. During the invite, Pastor Brown asked us where we stood with Christ and did our Pastor preach the true Word of God. We were backslidden, yet, I knew the Word of God because I had been gloriously saved at my last base in Osan, Korea in 1975.

My friend was just religious. Pastor Brown told us that if our pastor was not preaching the Word we needed to leave that church or he would come there and tell the pastor that he was not preaching the Word. When Pastor Brown left, my friend and I fell on the floor and laughed because this was the man that had 7 or 8 kids that my friend was telling me about. We said to each other, who does this man think he is saying he will tell another pastor that he is not preaching the Word? The next day was Sunday. Pastor Brown's words haunted us that night. I rededicated my life back to Christ, and we both tried to remember the directions to Pastor Brown's church. That is where I met Vera Brown, welcoming me to New Life Bible Church, Sumter, South Carolina. I met her 4 children not 7 or 8: Paulie, Carmela, Patrick, and Renita. They became family to me, and Vera invited me to her home. She lived right down the street. Vera explained to me that she was a stay-at-home mother and did not allow her children to attend parent homes that she did not know. My 2 sons, Andre and Juan, became friends with the Brown's children. Andre

Treasured Memories

and Patrick reconnected as adults in Columbus, Ohio and reconnected me back to the Brown family.

Vera as a wife was unbelievable. She always spoke to us referring to her husband as Pastor. Many times we wondered if he was her husband or pastor. Her example caused us to reverence Pastor Paul Brown even more. Pastor Brown was kind, but you could tell he was no nonsense. I am a very humorous and funny person. Pastor Brown's first informal one minute observation of me was the laughing which fooled everyone but him. I laughed to keep from crying for the sake of my sanity and the well-being of my children. Vera's love for Pastor Brown gave me hope for a good marriage which I persuaded myself I had, and my husband showed me I did not have. Vera required the women of New Life Bible Church to be good examples. She found out I was driving without a license and explained to me how I was bringing shame on God, the church, and Pastor Brown as my leader. My thoughts were, "I was not a member of New Life Bible Church," but because I attended there, she felt it was her and the ladies' responsibility to help me get my license. So, I tried many times and always failed. Just before I went to Eielson AFB, Alaska, I returned to Georgia and drove around the block, backed up and got my license after years of "riding dirty."

Vera encouraged us to love our husbands and children. Vera Brown was a champion woman. She lives on in her children. I especially see her in the face of her elder daughter, Carmela. Vera Brown was an excellent example of loving and living the Word. Vera's smile spoke volumes and when she spoke and she always did, she would make you feel that you were touched by an angel of God. I am glad that I met her. Vera Brown touched my life, and I grew.

Verlena Oliver Hawkins

I Love My Sister

I love my sister Vera so very much. I have several memorable moments, but my fondest is when I was a child. Vera taught me how to play several childhood games, such as, jump rope, double dutch, orange dutch, platt the may pole, jack stones, and pick-up sticks. Of course, she won all of the games.

Another memorable moment was when I was attending Trident Tech for my CAN certification. I remember failing my final exam. When I called to tell Paul that I did not pass the exam, Vera was on the phone as well. I said, hi to her, but she did not respond. As I began to tell Paul that I did not pass the course, Vera heard me. She said, "That's ok. You go back and take the course again. You will pass it. Study hard, ask questions, write down notes, make sure that you study real well before you take the test again, and you will pass it."

I did exactly what she said, and I passed the test. Now I have been a Certified Nurse's Assistant for 7 seven years. I did call Paul and Vera back and told them that I passed. Vera said, "I told you that you can do it." Thank you, my dearest sister, for encouraging me to go back to school. I love you and miss you so much, Vera.

Twin Sister Joyce Joyner

I'll Always Remember Vera Brown

I first met beautiful Vera Brown who shined inward and outward. It was around the late 70's. Vera was teaching a women's bible study from a booklet entitled "A Gracious Woman." We met in the living room of Paul and Vera Brown's home every Friday night. I became a part of the Bible study with a broken heart, painful, and confused, but with growing hope that God was going to heal my marriage after a recent separation from my husband.

I was new in Christ, and I looked forward to the weekly Bible study. It was like Vera had taken me under her wings to nurture me, and she aided me in my spiritual growth. I did not realize how much I needed a closer walk with Christ until the bible study enhanced my growth.

Each study started with weekly bible verse memorization. Hiding God's Word in my heart so that I would not sin against Him (Psalm 119:11)! Memorization was a challenge for me, but Vera's consistency made it very rewarding. I did not only memorize His Word but spoke God's Word believing that His Word would come to pass. I learned to apply God's Word to my daily life. The broken heart, pain, and confusion became a part of my testimony and the healing began through God's Word.

Vera always encouraged us to study and memorize our verses daily. I hungered for God's Word. I desired to grow. I wanted to remain faithful to our Lord and Savior. This came through the bible study. It was so very instrumental in my Christian walk and leading family members to Christ.

I was very touched by the wonderful, never seen before, family Christ-like example, in the Brown's home. Vera as a Christian, wife, mother, and friend, gave me a new look on life. My existence was new and different in Christ. I had no doubt that GOD was already healing my marriage even though James and I were thousands of miles apart. The miles did not matter. GOD was making the difference.

Part of my testimony, I still share and appreciate how being under Vera's teachings helped developed me as a Christian, wife, mother, daughter, and friend. I am so grateful God allowed me to be in Vera's life and she in mine.

God healed my marriage and we grew together for 46 years. I have loved and respected Vera and I miss her. I will always remember Vera Brown.

Annette B. Thompson

Charm is deceitful, and beauty is vain, but a woman who fears the Lord is to be praised." Proverbs 31:30

Vera, along with her husband, Dr. Paul Brown, shared their love for Christ with all who would listen. Vera was a person who feared the Lord. She was kind, thoughtful, giving, and a caring woman of God, who always put family, the church, and others before herself. She was quiet but was full of wisdom. She stood up for what was right and would not settle for anything less! My husband and I will always remember the respect she had for the man of God, but what made the biggest impression on me was the way she always made it a point to include me (his wife) with that same respect as her First Lady.

I will always remember how Vera knew when I was reaching my spiritual drain and needed my spirit refreshed. She would always say something to lift my spirit. Vera decided to send me (along with the church) to Dallas, Texas to attend the Tony Evans, "First Lady Conference." Vera knew the modesty in me would never accept such a gift, so she was so persistent and insisted, until I finally said yes! Vera knew and understood the importance of being around the spiritual support system that other First Ladies would be able to offer. That conference provided me with everything she thought it would and more! My spirit was filled, and I returned renewed and refreshed. I will forever be indebted to her and her ability to listen to God and move when He spoke.

Vera shared her thoughts on marriage and family and was a perfect example of what she taught. She was truly a person who was respected, that you could look up and listen to. I thank God for the opportunity to have shared time, laughter, dinners, prayers, and sisterhood with such a godly woman, who God placed in my life for a while, but made an impact, I will never forget.

Dr. Sareta Brown

I Appreciated Mrs. Vera

Thanks for taking the time out of your busy schedule to be with me. I told my Mom at the last minute of an event that I need an adult to attend with me. Mom hadn't made preparation to be off her job. She went to thinking as whom she could get to stand in for her. She said maybe Mrs. Vera will if she asks and she did. Mrs. Vera came to my school and was my Mom for about 2 hours. I will never forget her for taking that time to be with me.

Love is true, Love is divine
Put this on your heart
Keep it on your mind
Jesus is love, This we know
Sow good seeds, But not for show
Love yea one another as Jesus loves us all.

Emma and Tiffany Rhodes

I am pleased to share in expressing my heartfelt appreciation concerning the fellowship with Vera, my spiritual sister. Her smile is a vivid picture in my memory. It illuminated the joy that flooded her heart. One of our personal sharing times included a visit on a Friday evening to my home. There were no interruptions. As we shared, I developed closeness with my sister that came as a result of her sharing about the love she was endowed with from the Lord. I saw that genuine love being lived out through serving her husband, children, family and people in general. I was encouraged and could relate because we both understood that loving others meant action more than words. To God be the glory!

Betty Prince, Omnipotent God Ministries

I met Vera through her husband Paul Brown in 1993. I was stationed at Maxwell Air Force Base, Montgomery, AL. Vera Brown was a strong woman of faith in Christ Jesus. One of her favorite phrases that impacted my life was "Just do what God says." Vera influenced me in many ways, especially as a Christian wife and mother to her children. First, she submitted herself to Christ and to His authority. Secondly, she submitted herself to the authority of her own husband, Paul Brown. She had many qualities of a virtuous woman found in Proverbs 31. Vera worked with Paul in ministries. She was an industrial woman whose candle never went out. Her life was far above rubies. Her children grew up and called her blessed. I encourage you to read this book. This book explains how Vera Brown walked with God as a woman of faith.

It's all about Jesus (Acts 1:8)!

Freddie Prince, Omnipotent God Ministries

REMEMBERING MY VERA BROWN

To know Vera Brown is to love her. I can truly say that until I really got to know Vera, I thought she was a bit standoffish. Her husband, Dr. Paul Brown, was warm and effusive from the moment I laid eyes on the family at Canaan Hill Missionary Baptist Church in Montgomery, Alabama. I knew there was something different about this family when they introduced themselves that Sunday morning, but I didn't know the effect they, especially Vera, would have on my life. What I took for aloofness was the evidence of someone being watchful as well as prayerful. Vera seemed to have eyes that went everywhere. She did not miss a thing that was going on around her. I am from Montgomery, but had not lived there in a long time, so I felt out of place around people that I had grown up with. I had experienced and seen things that made me view the world differently.

Because we had shared experiences, I naturally wanted to be around her. She didn't seem to really notice me at first, but I knew she saw me. As I said before, Vera Brown didn't miss a thing. I was drawn by her grace, elegance, and calm demeanor. (I found out later that she was full of the fire of the Holy Ghost.) I made it my business to talk with her every chance I got because I knew she had something I needed. Finally, one Sunday the girls and I were invited to dinner. I was elated and talked with the girls about being on their best behavior so we could get a chance to visit again. This was the beginning of our friendship. After that, we spent many Saturday and Sunday afternoons at the Browns' home both in Montgomery and Millbrook. The lessons that I learned from Vera about being a godly mother and friend were invaluable. I watched with awe at how she calmed David when he was upset. I listened to her talk to Renita, Shay, and Erica about being young ladies and how to carry themselves. Although, my girls had four aunts in Montgomery at the time, Vera stepped right in and was like a fifth aunt who poured into their lives physically and spiritually.

I will always remember Vera telling me that you had to cover your husband in prayer, especially when they are in ministry. I know that she continually prayed for Pastor Paul and was very particular about who she allowed into their realm of influence. I can remember walking with them in street ministry and knocking on doors. One of my strongest memories involved her trusting me as a sister in Christ to go and minister to a young lady one Sunday afternoon. The girls and I were with the Browns, and Pastor Paul received the call from Senior Pastor Ossie Brown that one of the members needed to be ministered to. She had just had a baby, and her husband was missing. This lady just happened to be a close friend of mine. I remember Vera telling me that I should go with Pastor Paul because of my relationship with the young lady. She could have easily told me that I needed to go home so that she and Pastor Paul could go and minister, but because she listened to God's Spirit and she "knew" me and knew I was about my Father's business, Vera sent me on assignment to go minister.

I have so many fond memories of Vera. I miss her friendship, our walks, our talks, her grace, her beauty, her wisdom, etc. I could go on and on, but the truth of the matter is, "I JUST MISS VERA".

Costella Edwards

Chapter 9

THE WORD OF GOD HAS NO EXPIRATION DATE

"The grass withereth, the flower fadeth: but the Word of our God shall stand forever." Isaiah 40:8

As I reflect on a life well-lived, I thank God for the life and legacy of Vera L. Brown. She contributed significantly to the body of Christ and desired people be saved. It was a joy serving our Savior together. I count it all joy to have been chosen for us to spend a lifetime together.

God has given me such great memories over our 50 plus years together. Through the years I recall our days in high school, when we were married, as we raised five godly seeds who are sowing into the kingdom, as we battled together the ups and downs of the Christian life, and as we traveled around the globe making a difference for Christ wherever we went, the many souls we were privileged to disciple. So much more could be said. However, I can honestly say that we desired to do what God said. We acted on the promises of God. Now she is a part of that great cloud of witnesses cheering us on to keep pressing. One of these days we believers in Jesus will be reunited for all eternity.

I have come to know that God is Jehovah-nissi, the Lord our banner, and we can go from triumph to triumph and say, "Thanks be to God who has given us the victory through our Lord Jesus Christ" (1 Corinthians 15:57). The Word of God does not have an expiration date, and we believed every word that God wrote.

The Apostle Paul's letter to the church in Rome states, "For whatever things were written before were written for our learning, that we through the patience and comfort of the Scriptures might have hope (Romans 15:4). As we read the biblical account of the patriarchs and believers in Scripture, we learn of their response to the word of God. The success and victories they achieved were because they did what God required. The underlying theme was one of obedience. It is the same today and does not get old. The principles of Scripture are still applicable to any generation. I highly encourage everyone to stay aligned with the will of God by doing what He has commanded. The result leads to a Christ-centered life.

It is my hope that you have been encouraged, gain some insights, and obtained some nuggets because of reading this book. I have learned to rest in the promises of God. He is faithful. "Your lovingkindness, O Lord, extends to the heavens, Your faithfulness reaches to the skies" (Psalm 36:5). I am reminded: Do not keep it to yourself; appropriate the principles of God, and share them with others. I can hear Vera saying, "*Just Do What God Says.*"

CPSIA information can be obtained
at www.ICGtesting.com
Printed in the USA
FSHW022042260721
83500FS